YOU'RE MAKING OTHER PEOPLE RICH

You're Making Other People Rich

SAVE, INVEST, & SPEND
WITH INTENTION

Ryan Sterling

LIONCREST
PUBLISHING

YOU'RE MAKING OTHER PEOPLE RICH

Save, Invest, and Spend with Intention

ISBN   978-1-5445-0751-4 *Hardcover*

        978-1-5445-0749-1 *Paperback*

        978-1-5445-0750-7 *Ebook*

For Lauren, there is no way any of this
would be possible without you.

Contents

Introduction

Broke, depressed, and on the verge of divorce, I was bottoming out.

No one could tell.

As the newly minted senior vice president at an investment management firm, I had a mid-six-figure income and a life full of pleasure and convenience. If you spent five minutes with me, you'd be convinced that everything was great—mostly because I needed to convince myself that everything was all good.

In fact, everything was far from good. It wasn't supposed to be this way. I'd done everything the "right way." I wasn't perfect, but I knew damn well how to fall in line and deliver on expectations. I'd accomplished everything I set out to, and then some. My résumé told the story: degrees from highly rated schools, a Wall Street career, a fancy title, top industry designations, a high income, frequent fine dining, custom suits, a luxury downtown apartment, and limited life failures. On paper, I embodied the image of a successful professional. In secret, I was financially broke and suffering in silence.

I wish I could pinpoint the moment, or epiphany, when everything transformed. The moment when you clearly hit bottom, dust yourself off, and an inspirational montage (cue the music) fuels the engine for sustainable, positive change. The moment when you go from bad to good, from down-and-out to champion, from naïve to enlightened. In other words, I wish I could tell you that my turnaround was fast, easy, and triumphant. It wasn't. My turnaround was slow, methodical, and involved a lot of deep work.

I can map my turnaround through a series of turning points, like the time I realized I'd hit the "number." Just a decade earlier, I'd decided on an income threshold to represent my "I-made-it number." But once I made it, nothing changed. What I thought would be an exciting revelation was a depressing moment. Overconsumption caused me to be as financially insecure as ever, and even at that number I was still dependent on the next paycheck and bonus. I worked to finance my lifestyle but was missing out on life.

I remember looking at my credit card debt with horror and disgust. Instead of doing something about it, I ignored it, and put my focus and energy on something else. Intellectually, I knew this approach was foolish, but my ego was more powerful than my intellect. My ego was destroying my life, including my marriage to my wife, Lauren.

Lauren is my love, my partner. When we set out, we were each other's biggest cheerleaders. I've experienced more fun and laughter with her with than anyone else in the world and more joy than I ever imagined. But we became adversaries. I remember the turning point when it was clear that our marriage was on the brink of ending. We were sitting on the couch the morning after a night of rich food and cocktails (again), when we said the word *divorce* for the first time. The pursuit of money and the ideal lifestyle were making us unhealthy physically and emotionally. Our so-called dreams were tearing us apart. It wasn't immediately clear, but the life we'd created was based on unintentional consumption, actions, and choices—a life neither of us wanted.

We wanted to be a team. We wanted more purpose and meaning. We wanted financial independence.

Does any of this sound familiar? Are societal pressures and influences getting the best of you financially? Is your ego defeating your intellect? Is fear impeding action?

If you're waiting for that financial epiphany, it may never come. The truth is, most of us are in a chronic state of financial and personal misery. How do we self-medicate? We consume. Consumption provides a short-term dose of pleasure. It makes us feel happy and feeds the ego. It's a way to show others and prove to ourselves that we matter. It also provides a sense of control and the authority we crave to quiet our inner fears. But chronic, compulsory overconsumption is like a disease, keeping us trapped in a lifestyle full of unintentional choices and outcomes—a self-created prison.

The downward spiral was a slow burn. It could have gone on forever, but the actions we chose when faced with a series of turning points led to our commitment to a life of intention—where money was no longer a controlling or defining force but a resource in our pursuit of true desires, aspirations, and goals. We reached a place where physical and emotional health offered wealth that transcended money. A place where love, acceptance, and joy created meaning and abundance. Lauren and I never organized or "white-boarded" our way to this place, but looking back, our journey out of the financial pain and misery we created is clearly defined through awareness, accountability, and action.

AWARENESS (YOU'RE BEING EXPLOITED)

Awareness is the recognition that you're being exploited to consume *now*. This right now kind of culture is a detriment to your financial future. Awareness is the understanding that your innate desires for pleasure and convenience can inhibit personal growth. Awareness is the acknowledgment that you're made to feel like you live in a state of perceived scarcity and understanding how the scarcity mindset attracts poor financial decisions.

ACCOUNTABILITY (YOU CAN FIGHT BACK)

Accountability is defining what you want out of life and what you're willing to do for it. Are you ready to confront and disarm your ego, commit to change, and believe you can pursue meaning and purpose? Accountability is detaching from the things, outcomes, and beliefs that led you down the path to mindless consumption and unintentional choices.

ACTION (YOU CAN TAKE ACTION)

Action means paying off debt, building an emergency savings account, and creating and working toward meaningful goals. Action is not about being perfect, fast results, or pleasure. Action is about commitment, seeing progress, and celebrating success, while being resilient during setbacks.

Action leads to freedom.

PAST, PRESENT, AND FUTURE VERSIONS OF YOU (ME)

I love personal finance and investing, and I've been helping people save, invest, and reach their financial and personal goals for more than fifteen years. I've worked at some of the largest firms in the world and have advised everyone from retired teachers to billionaires. The irony is not lost on me—I was great at my job and advising others but horrible at managing my own money.

For the longest time, I was convinced that managing wealth was all about being technically sound, but there's much more to it than checking off boxes. Creating a net worth statement, building a budget, developing and implementing an investment strategy, reviewing insurance options, and planning for college were all important, but I learned the hard way that building wealth is less about the *how* and more about the *why* and *what*. Why is building wealth important? Why is it so hard to fight the urge to consume? Why does my ego control me? What do I want? What am I willing to commit to? When you understand why and what it takes, it's easier to build your awareness, be accountable, and spark action.

This book is for the person struggling to build wealth. It's for the person who feels trapped by money, ego, and expectations. It's for those suffering in silence who feel imprisoned by money and societal pressures, who crave financial and personal independence. In many ways, this book was written for the past version of me, but this book is also for the current and future versions of me. Building wealth is not an event, and it's not about some magic number; it's a personal, ongoing, dynamic, and ever-evolving process.

This book is not intended for the person who wants to get rich quick. Nor is it meant for the person who wants to "geek out" over numbers and projections, or those who demand perfection. The wealth-building process requires deep personal work and won't always be easy.

This book is not a story about my own personal and

financial journey, but I will share the process Lauren and I used to achieve financial independence. I'll also provide a handful of case studies from my fifteen-year career as a financial advisor (names have been altered to protect the privacy and confidentiality of clients throughout this book).

Are you tired of making other people rich? If you're ready to develop an awareness about how you're being exploited to mindlessly consume; be accountable to detach from the things, outcomes, and beliefs that have defined (and confined) you up to this point; and take action toward financial independence, please join us on this journey.

Wealth, abundance, and intention are waiting for you!

Part 1

You're Being Exploited

I Want It Now

"I think my generation is obsessed with instant gratification. We want everything now, now, now."

—DAKOTA FANNING

Do you want one marshmallow now, or two in fifteen minutes?

The late psychologist Dr. Walter Mischel and his colleagues posed this question to a group of children in his groundbreaking 1960s study on delayed gratification at Stanford University.[1] Two-thirds of the children elected to take one marshmallow immediately, but this finding was just the start. Later known as "the marshmallow test," Dr. Mischel gained further insight into delayed gratification several decades later when he followed

---

1   Jeannette L. Nolen, "Walter Mischel," *Encyclopaedia Britannica*, September 8, 2019, https://www.britannica.com/biography/Walter-Mischel.

up with the children. The results were staggering. The third of children who waited the entire fifteen minutes were demonstrably more successful (as measured by grades, test scores, self-worth, maturity, etc.) than the remaining two-thirds who had succumbed to temptation (instant gratification).

The ability to delay gratification led to higher levels of competence in dealing with stress, anxiety, and unhealthy cravings. Each extra minute preschoolers delayed the temptation of eating the marshmallow resulted in a 0.2 percent reduction in body mass index, thirty years later.

WHAT DRIVES OUR NEED FOR INSTANT GRATIFICATION?

There is a battle going on in your brain between your "hot system" and "cool system." Popularized by Dr. Mischel and his team, your hot system drives emotion and impulse and your cool system fuels your ability to reason and rationalize. Your hot system is controlled by the amygdala, the part of your brain that is easily triggered by stress and stimulus, while your cool system is controlled by the prefrontal cortex, the part of your brain that is responsible for executive functions—reason, decision making, and self-control.

Your hot system loves instant gratification. It wants you to buy those shoes now and worry about the consequences later. Your cool system tries to stop you. It uses reason and logic and reminds you of your long-term goals. While the systems are both important parts of being a whole and healthy person, when it comes to spending, your cool system is at a major disadvantage. Why? Because of distance, intention, and imagination.

DISTANCE

Long-term goals are distant and abstract. You can't see, touch, or taste them. Current consumption is right in front of you, and you can experience the benefit today. The closer you are to the reward, the greater the advantage to your hot system. Your cool system knows that building wealth is a priority, but when it comes to making a decision between buying a beautiful pair of shoes or saving for retirement, your long-term goals are no match. The distance is too far. You're buying the shoes.

INTENTION

Why do we act on impulse and emotion? It's likely because we have no clue what we really want. We have no direction or intention. We're just moving through life reacting to the stimuli around us. Bright lights, models, and sale signs draw us in, and before our cool system has a chance to process what's happening, our hot system is swiping the credit card. Our hot system is spending with little to no consideration of whether the purchase gets us closer to, or further away from, our values and true wants.

IMAGINATION

For your cool system to be effective, you need to be willing and able to imagine the future. Your brain needs to visualize how good the end of the journey will feel by delaying consumption. With the noise and distractions that occupy our lives, our attention is under attack. It's nearly impossible to step back and imagine the benefits that come with waiting. Our brains are too cluttered.

To make things even harder on your cool system, brands and marketers are well aware of its vulnerabilities and do all they can to diminish its influence.

BRAND/MARKETING STRATEGIES

Each day you're exposed to between four thousand to ten thousand brand messages. Each message has the same goal: to get you to buy now! These people behind these brands are clever and appeal to your hot system because they know it's in control.

"NOW" MESSAGING

"Lose ten pounds in ten days!" Think of the power behind this message. It promises a real benefit in a short period of time.

The real brilliance comes when a message can tug at both your hot and cool systems. Your hot system is being targeted with a promise for a short-term reward (it will only take ten days), while your cool system is being targeted by a sensible goal (lose ten pounds). Deep down, your cool system can detect when something's too good to be true, but it's also exhausted from the constant resistance. So, it lays down and waits for a different battle. This explains why schemes to get rich quick and expensive products to lose weight fast can be so effective.

SALES AND PROMOTIONS

Study the sales and promotions that crowd your inbox. What are they trying to tell you?

The thing you want is on sale *now*, and it's going fast.

There's no time to wait. You're immediately flooded with concern that you're going to miss out on something you want, and at a good price. You don't trust that the sale will be available in the future. Time constraints provide little time and space for your cool system to catch up with your hot system's desire to act. Forget about your long-term goals and values. Forget about intention because time is running out.

IMAGERY

Brand experts have done an amazing job doing the imagining for us. They sell us clothes using models that look the way we want to look. They don't just show us a picture of a chair; they show us what our entire living room could look like. They don't show us a can of paint; they show us how beautiful our entire house will look with a new color scheme. Our cool system is no match.

To make matters worse, brands and marketers know when to get you.

How? Because you're telling them. They know what you like, who you like, how you like it, and when you want it. And they know when you're most vulnerable. There is an old marketing saying: "You waste half of your marketing budget; the only problem is you don't know which half." Yet, with social media, online search, and digital advertising, this is no longer the case. Your digital footprint is all over the internet. Data is now the most valuable commodity in the world, and these companies are the keepers. We may not be able to avoid social media and the internet completely, but we can be more mindful of our vulnerabilities as they relate to the manipulation of our actions and intentions.

GROWTH OF CREDIT

Once you have an engaged customer, reduce any friction between the customer and the sale. This is the first rule of sales. In retail, the main friction points used to be traveling to a physical store and having cash to make a purchase. This is no longer the case. With the explosion of credit cards and e-commerce, there is zero distance between you and the sale. The easier they make it on you, the more you spend. You want it now, and you can have it now. This is terrible for your cool system. As a result, consumer debt levels are at a peak—the average American owes $6,849 in credit card debt.[2] And with credit card interest rates as high as 25 percent, the average American is paying up to $100 each month in credit card interest alone.

---

2   Erin El Issa, "2019 American Household Credit Card Debt Study," NerdWallet, December 2, 2019, https://www.nerdwallet.com/blog/average-credit-card-debt-household/.

Think of interest as the cost of access to extra money. You are paying for the right to use an intangible, excess resource. When you're caught in a spiral of debt, interest can make the hole even deeper.

For most banks, the credit card division is a multibillion-dollar industry with a goal of collecting a lifetime of interest from you. We can't help ourselves, and they oblige by making spending as easy as possible. When you act on an impulse using credit, just remember this: you must pay it back. If you can't pay it back in full, the interest will cost you.

CAN YOU TRAIN YOURSELF TO EMBRACE DELAYED GRATIFICATION?

Instant gratification is saying yes to mindless consumption. It's succumbing to the daily attacks of brand messages and allowing yourself to be manipulated to spend. Delayed gratification is the exact opposite. It's about being committed to your goals, living in alignment with your values, and imagining all the benefits that come with waiting and prioritizing to build the future version of you. It will take time, but you can train yourself to embrace delayed gratification. It all comes down to giving your cool system a louder and more commanding voice. When your cool system is in control, you are saving, investing, and spending with intention. And intention is the difference between working toward meaningful goals as opposed to owning a lot of stuff.

We'll cover this in more detail in upcoming chapters, but here is a sneak preview and some helpful tips and tricks to help you fight back against the urge to consume:

BRING FUTURE GOALS TO THE PRESENT.

While saving for retirement is an important goal, it's too far away. The only way we'll embrace saving and budgeting is if we can get some points on the board today. We need to see progress. We need savings goals and targets that are within reach. We need to shorten the distance. Building wealth is like training for a marathon—start small, celebrate the early wins, and slowly increase the distance.

CREATE SPACE BETWEEN THE IMPULSE AND ACTION.

Doing some impulsive online shopping? Before checking out, try stepping away for at least five minutes. Create some distance between the impulse to consume and the purchase. Doing so will allow time and space for you to think about the fact that you're letting go of your hard-earned dollars and making somebody else rich. *Everyone's getting paid, except you.* Remind yourself of this. You may still make the purchase, but there will at least be some thought and intention behind the action.

ALTER YOUR ENVIRONMENT.

If you struggle with overconsumption in times of stress and anxiety, remove the ability to consume.

Did you just get paid? Great! Now, pay yourself first. Move a set amount to a savings account after each paycheck. Because when it's out of your checking account, you are less prone to spend it.

Feeling anxious and looking to calm your nerves through some online shopping? Try taking your nervous energy to the gym. A two-mile run or a yoga class will help clear your mind, and by the time you're done, the impulse to consume will be long gone.

Succumbing to another promotional email? Unsubscribe from the mailing list.

Can't resist stopping at the mall after a difficult day at the office? Change your route home. Eliminate temptation.

KNOW YOUR VALUES.

What do you want at a deep level? Do you even know? If not, work on defining your values and goals. The next time you find yourself ready to consume, ask yourself: "Does this purchase align with my values or get me closer to my goals?" Once you have the answer, you'll know if it's right to move forward. Visualize the best version of yourself. What does your best life look like, and how does the purchase fit into it? If you are a visual person, try putting together a vision board and place it in an area where you will see it every day. If you are online or like apps, you can also use Pinterest.

Do whatever you can to have daily reminders of your goals, values, and true wants.

UNDERSTAND THE PLEASURE PRINCIPLE.

Fighting back against mindless consumption is all about creating more meaning and purpose elsewhere in your life because meaning, not consumption, is the real secret to fulfillment. As we age, we often lose touch with personal growth, an area of life that brings the greatest amount of meaning.

We settle into a daily routine and by the time we get home from work, we value pleasure and convenience above all else. We're paying a high price for the pleasure and convenience, though: it's making us depressed, overweight, and broke.

CHAPTER 2

In Need of Pleasure

"When you first arrive, you wear white T-shirts every day. Once you survive Hell Week, you get to swap them out for brown shirts. It was a symbol that we'd advanced to a higher level, and after a lifetime of mostly failure, I definitely felt like I was someplace new."

—DAVID GOGGINS, *CAN'T HURT ME: MASTER YOUR MIND AND DEFY THE ODDS*

In his memoir, David Goggins (quite possibly the toughest human on the planet) details the physical and mental challenges he faced during Navy Seal training. Each year, roughly one thousand candidates start Navy Seal training, but only 20 percent finish. Most exit during the infamous Hell Week—a week full of back-to-back challenges with little to no sleep. It took David three attempts, but he made it through and went on to have a decorated military career.

While there are countless lessons to learn from reading *Can't Hurt Me*, I'll expound on the small detail highlighted in the quote I shared about swapping out the white shirts for brown, and break down the meaning behind it. But first, let's talk about a deadly pursuit: the pursuit of pleasure.

PLEASURE

As a society, we're addicted to pleasure. According to Douglas J. Lisle, PhD and Alan Goldhamer, DC, authors of *The Pleasure Trap: Mastering the Hidden Force that Undermines Health & Happiness*, all animals (including humans) are hardwired to pursue pleasure, avoid pain, and conserve energy. Our hardwiring is killing us. Our society is depressed, overweight, and broke.

Statistics reveal that:

- Depression is now the leading cause of disability worldwide.[3]

---

3   "Depression," World Health Organization, December 4, 2019, https://www.who.int/news-room/fact-sheets/detail/depression.

- 40 percent of US adults are obese.[4]
- 69 percent of Americans have less than $1,000 in savings.[5]

As highlighted in the last chapter, brands and marketers know how to exploit our innate instincts. In the case of appealing to our pleasure sensors, it all comes down to getting a dopamine release.

Dopamine is the feel-good hormone. It's activated when we're in striking distance of a reward. When it's released, you feel euphoria and bliss. You know when it's activated. Healthy activities that trigger a dopamine response include exercising, feeling love, and achieving goals. Unhealthy activities include drug abuse, gambling, eating unhealthy treats, and shopping.

On the food front, dopamine release comes down to three words: sugar, salt, and fat. As a result, we have access to cheap, quick snacks that are full of empty calories and hollow pleasure that are making us fat. On the shopping front, we get our dopamine fix from buying something new that makes us feel good and

---

4   "Adult Obesity Facts," Centers for Disease Control and Prevention, https://www.cdc.gov/obesity/data/adult.html.

5   John Csiszar, "Best Savings Accounts of 2020," December 3, 2019, Go Banking Rates, https://www.gobankingrates.com/saving-money/savings-advice/americans-have-less-than-1000-in-savings/.

excited. We deserve it, right? However, it doesn't take long before the "high" of consumption wears off. Soon, the new thing becomes old stuff. And we quickly start to get the itch to buy something new. It's an expensive cycle that always gets us back to the same place: wanting more.

PAIN AVOIDANCE

The teams behind brands know about our desire to avoid pain, so they make consumption easy. They hold brainstorming sessions to figure out every possible way to ease our pain points with haste. How else do you think we got online checkouts, easy pay apps and solutions, credit cards, and the ability to pay through your watch or wave a card to buy your coffee? How does it feel when you take actual cash out of your wallet? Do you pause for a second? Does it feel like you're letting go of something important? It should, because you are. Paying with cash is painful. How does it feel when you swipe your credit card or pay with your watch? Do you feel anything at all? The pain is delayed and easy to ignore. Why? Because the pain is a problem for "Future You."

CONSERVATION OF ENERGY

Brands know that we're instinctively lazy, so they've

rigged the supply chain to make delivery easy. If you can walk from your couch to your door, you can have anything you want. This pleasure trap has tricked us into embracing a life full of consumption. It's a negative feedback loop that feeds itself. It's depressing, unhealthy, and needs to stop.

A PERFECT DAY OF PLEASURE, PAIN AVOIDANCE, AND ENERGY CONSERVATION

Imagine a day where we act on all three of these innate instincts. It would look something like this: sitting on a couch eating ice cream while shopping online, ordering unhealthy food for delivery, alternating between watching movies and playing video games (all dopamine releasing activities that involve little pain). Does this sound like a fulfilling day? You're meant for so much more! At some point, Lauren and I realized the detriment of the pleasure trap in our lives and we began taking small steps to reconnect to pain.

HOW DID THIS HAPPEN?

Humans sought pleasure over everything and ended our relationship with pain, but the pleasure overload blocked our clarity on the necessity of pain. With pain comes growth. Learning to love and embrace pain develops physical and mental muscles that allow us to push through new challenges and pursue more meaningful opportunities. It pushes us past our previous limits of what we thought was possible. It builds character and confidence.

When you're settled into a comfortable job and lifestyle, the idea of introducing pain into a life of pleasure and convenience sounds ridiculous. That said, there are times in your life when you have no choice but to accept and embrace pain. I'd argue that, in every instance, growth follows.

THE EARLY YEARS

Remember your early years? Think about the growth you experienced from infancy to turning ten years old. Now think of the years between eleven and twenty-two. Your life was all about personal growth. Things that are easy now were once major challenges you confronted and conquered. You couldn't rest on the knowledge you have today because it was still being formed. You were busy learning, exploring, experimenting, and embracing new activities. You learned how to win and lose. In many ways, your life was full of discomfort and uncertainty. During this period of trial and error, your life was full of unanswered questions.

ADULT YEARS—LESS PAIN, MORE COMFORT

With each new growth stage, we settle into our interests, hone our skills, and work on our talents. With every step, we grow closer to our ultimate goals of feeling safe and having it all figured out. We get married, achieve a prestigious title in our chosen career, buy a house, have kids...We plant our flag in this world and imagine we have life's questions answered. We feel secure, or at least we have the sense that we're secure.

Let me introduce you to someone else who thought he was secure in his pursuits. We'll call him Mike.

CASE STUDY: MIKE, THE BORED ACCOUNTANT

Mike did everything the "right way." Good grades in high school led to a competitive college, which landed him a job at a major accounting firm. By the time he was in his early thirties, he had progressed in his life and career. He was making six figures, married with two kids, and paying a hefty mortgage on a beautiful home. He settled into a routine, living the standard suburban lifestyle. Some would say, the American Dream.

He was a consumer of pleasure and suffered almost no pain. Life was comfortable. Comfort was silently killing him. Consistent consumption of overly-processed snacks at home and work, sitting at a desk, commuting from home to work in his car, and very little walking resulted in eighty pounds of excess weight. His routine led to stagnation. Stagnation gave way to boredom, which fueled him to indulge in expensive gadgets, toys, and "things" to keep him excited. He had no savings and carried steep credit card debt. He was trapped by the lifestyle.

When he asked for money advice, he expected a standard answer. Build a budget, pay off debt, and create an emergency savings account. While those elements all are important, I told him to do something else first.

I told him to get uncomfortable.

Take on some extra responsibilities at work, start a side hustle, sign up for a 10K race. I wanted him to try anything that seemed like a challenge, and a little scary. Before I share the results of Mike's challenge, I want to take you back a step to the quote from David Goggins and focus on the brown shirt.

MEANING VERSUS PLEASURE

Think about the pain, suffering, and doubt David experienced during Hell Week, all for the right to swap out a white shirt for a brown shirt. Hell Week was far from pleasure. So, why did he fight through it while most of his classmates tapped out?

Because graduating from Hell Week had meaning behind it.

Before Hell Week, he was bullied, abused, and overweight. After Hell Week, he was on his way to earning his spot in one of the most respected groups in the military.

Did the brown shirt have any material value? No!

If he went out wearing the plain brown shirt in public, would people look at him as a man of status? No!

Was it easy to get? Hell no!

The brown shirt had meaning. Meaning to him.

Does this mean we should quit our jobs and sign up to be a Navy Seal? For some, maybe. For the rest of us, it's a reminder that we need more brown shirts in our lives.

Your brown shirt could be a professional certification that will help your career. Sure, it may be hard to achieve and you may need to put in hours of self-study, but it will have meaning and perhaps spark a promotion.

What about the side hustle you've been dreaming of? You may need to work after-hours and on the weekend, but, over time, it could turn into your full-time profession, providing a reward far beyond money—meaning.

Maybe you desire an athletic achievement? You don't have to be a professional athlete to feel the thrill of competition. Think of a 10K, half-marathon, or marathon. The reward at the finish line isn't the medal. It's the meaning behind the achievement—knowing you put in the work and achieved something that seemed impossible.

None of these accomplishments cost much except a little bit of pain, time, and commitment, although the rewards are far beyond the material sacrifices.

So how did Mike the accountant's life change just by re-introducing pain? In less than a year, Mike volunteered to lead a firm-wide project, which led to a promotion and a raise. He started a daily walking routine, committed to cooking more at home, created a blog, and lost over thirty pounds. He curbed his consumption, is close to paying off his credit card debt, and is the happiest he's been in a long time. He feels like a better husband and father and is closer to being the person he always wanted to be.

It all started with getting uncomfortable.

Most of us already have an abundance of "stuff," when what we really need is an abundance of *meaning*.

CHAPTER 3

Scarcity in Times of Abundance

"It's not the man who has too little, but the man who craves more, that is poor."

—SENECA

We live in times of great abundance. We have "more" now than at any other point in human history. We have access to more technology, information, and medical breakthroughs. Our homes are bigger, we own more cars, and food is always present in large quantities. With so much abundance, why does it feel like we have so little?

SCARCITY MINDSET

The scarcity mindset is a zero-sum game.

If you have more than I do, you win, and I lose. The equation of 1 + -1 will always equal zero. Reality TV, social media, magazine ads, and billboards are all daily reminders of what we don't have. We're told there's only one way to win: consume. But the scarcity mindset is about so much more than winning and losing. At its core, the scarcity mindset is rooted in fear. It has origins going back thousands of years, to a time when food was scarce, and fear was an appropriate response. It was crucial for survival.

Fear is a powerful emotion. It's triggered when there is a perceived threat to physical or psychological safety. When our safety is in question, eliminating the threat becomes our number-one priority. Thus, fear captures our attention and takes us from a place of abundance (look at all the possibilities) to scarcity (look at how much I stand to lose). When it comes to consumption, the emotions that illicit the most fear surround losing or having less than others.

LOSS

Do you like the feeling of losing? I didn't think so. When it comes to consuming, nothing can get you to "act now" like the threat of losing out. Think about the last time you missed out on a major sale. It may still haunt you to this day. You experienced a missed opportunity. You lost, and worse than that, someone else won.

When you live in a state of mind where you're constantly worried about losing, fear is always present. To make matters worse, most of the triggers and outcomes that bring about the feeling of loss are beyond our control. We can't control retailers. We can't control our bosses. We can't control our relationships. So, we hold on to what we *can* control. We go into protector mode, avoid calculated risks, and we play to not lose. As a result, we place a greater value on our "stuff" and become extra vigilant over sales and promotions for more "stuff" we don't need. Worst of all, we instruct our ego to build a massive wall to separate us from any perceived threat of losing. This, in turn, prevents us from engaging in areas that bring about personal growth and development because the status quo represents safety.

LESS

How does it feel when you find out that a friend or colleague makes more money than you? Or when your friend shows up in a brand-new luxury car? Or when you see reality TV stars in mega-mansions?

"I have less!"

Is that what you say to yourself? If so, it can be a horrible feeling that makes you feel poor and cheated. "Why don't I have what they have?" In this time of plenty, how is it possible that we experience this emotion? It's because we're under attack with messages and images of people with more.

Brands pay celebrities and influencers to convince you that someone you follow (and think you know) has, or is experiencing, something fun and exciting, and you're missing out. Fear of missing out (or FOMO) is a powerful emotion. It doesn't matter how you feel about the celebrity, friend, or influencer. Whether you like, respect, or loathe them, the feeling is the same. You're missing out. You have so little.

Consumption lessens the threat in the short term. Once you have the thing, the danger of less is gone. It's only a temporary refrain because consuming "it" doesn't change the fact that it's just a "thing." You feel great for a moment only to move toward the next "thing" you don't have. It's a destructive cycle. This is no way to live.

ABUNDANCE

Thankfully, you have an opportunity to reframe the conversation. Missing out on that sale? Good! Your closet is full anyway, and that money can go toward something more meaningful. Friend or reality star showing off their new watch? Try being happy for them. You lost nothing.

You have a supercomputer in your pocket, access to a wealth of information in just one click, and cures to diseases that have wiped out previous generations. We live in an age of abundance, and adding more "stuff" is just clutter. Missing out on more "stuff" does you a favor. Missing out gives you back more time and space.

REFRAME YOUR EXPECTATIONS

Expectations drive the feelings of loss and having less because when you expect a certain outcome, you are focused on a win or a loss. Ask yourself why you have the expectation. Did you define the expectation? Did you do something to deserve the expected outcome? Did you want or expect this "thing" before seeing the ad or influencer? Was this "thing" missing in your life before you became aware of it?

You manufacture the ideas of loss and less. They are just thoughts. You can reframe the conversation to get out of the mental state of scarcity and to a place of abundance.

SAY "THANKS" MORE OFTEN

Financially secure and independent people make gratitude a daily practice. They stop and give thanks for the people, things, and experiences that add to their life. A great way to keep tabs on our blessings is by starting a gratitude journal. Take a moment daily to write down every blessing in your life, even if it's as simple as appreciating the absence of a catastrophe. There are so many negative events or outcomes that could be happening right now, but all is well. Celebrate that because if things were worse, you'd likely give anything to get back to your current state.

Try writing in your gratitude journal when you wake up in the morning, before bed, or at a random point throughout the day. You don't even need to write it down. Just get in a practice of saying, "Thanks." I'll let you in on a secret. *If you can't be thankful for everything you have right now, nothing will ever be enough.* Your life isn't perfect, but there's a lot to be thankful for if you just stop, think, and express your gratitude.

We all have the power to create paradise or prisons.

It all comes down to perception. You can be in paradise while waiting for a delayed flight, rationalizing with a screaming child, or walking in the pouring rain. You can be in misery after a $50,000 bonus, living in a mansion, or flying on a private jet.

Gratitude is paradise. It's your choice.

ABUNDANCE IN SIMPLICITY

Eliminating noise, temptation, and distractions can go a long way toward living a life of wealth and fulfillment.

We make an estimated thirty-five thousand decisions each day. That's over two thousand decisions each waking hour. Life is complicated, and with the speed of technology and information, it's only getting worse. Our time and mental capacity are under constant attack as we ponder decisions about food, clothes, education, career, investing, shopping, fitness, social media, and what to watch on TV. The solution seems to point toward doing and having more. Download a new productivity app. Buy a bigger house. Work longer hours. Watch and read more news. More stuff turns into more obligations, distractions, work, money, and stress. We're pulled in a million directions, and our time, intention, and attention are hostages held captive by the next decision.

We're expected to achieve. Get good grades. Get into a

certain school. Land the job. Move up the ranks. With each step comes a new set of expectations, complexity, and decisions. We have no time to think, no time to get lost in an experience, and no time to embrace the joy and abundance of simplicity. It's no wonder anxiety and depression are on the rise:

- You're being exploited to act on instant gratification.
- You're being exploited to overconsume in your pursuit of pleasure.
- You're being told you lost out on something new.
- You're being told you have less than someone else.

We spend most of our lives being told what to do. First, by our parents and then our teachers. We graduate, and our bosses tell us what to do and how to do it. Friends and family go on to tell us what we *should* be doing: You should buy a home. You should get married. You should have a child. You should have a "real" job. These are all suggestions based on what *they* do. Society tells us what we should value every day.

We grow attached to these expectations. They become our values, and they cause us to act without intention. We're led to believe that fulfillment is accomplished by meeting or exceeding these expectations. But these expectations are defined for us, not by us.

Just look around at most of your stuff. How much of it do you really value? Examine a typical day in your life. Are you being intentional with your time? With your money? I wasn't. I spent my money on activities and things that others told me to value, want, and need. I spent my time being told what to do because I was trapped by a lifestyle with expectations that were making me broke, unfulfilled, and unhealthy. I didn't need more knowledge. I didn't need more "stuff." I needed to gain abundance by simplifying my life and reframing my relationship with money, expectations, and values, on my terms.

You can gain an abundant thought process. You have power, but you must believe. It's time to fight back.

Part 2

You Can Fight Back

CHAPTER 4

What Do You Want?

"Complaining about a problem without posing a solution is called whining."

—THEODORE ROOSEVELT

How many of your friends and family are in a never-ending cycle of complaints? You might be included in that number. In fact, you probably are. It's estimated that the average person complains thirty times a day. Complaining is like a call you don't want to take on your smartphone. We hit "ignore" mentally because we're all tired of hearing and listening to a constant barrage of grumblings. It sounds harsh, but it's true. In a way, you could say that too much complaining is one of my biggest complaints. See how easy it is?

Money is particularly ripe for complaints. We complain that we have too little, that we make too little, or that somebody else makes too much. We complain that lack of money holds us back from engaging in more meaningful opportunities and experiences or that we're tied to a job, location, or relationship because we can't afford to break away. The reality is, most of us spend a lifetime complaining and worrying about money.

It doesn't have to be this way. We all have an opportunity to change our relationship with money and to see money as a resource, not a roadblock. For most of us, when we think about the things that will make us happy, we define a material want. "I want a luxury car!" "I want a designer watch!" "I want a bigger house!" Next, we examine our financial resources. "Do I have the money?" If yes, we buy it. If no, we either wait for a raise, bonus, or gift, or we buy it on credit (with interest costs). We continue through this cycle and sometimes we're happy or sad, but we're always under the control and mercy of our temptations, insecurities, and bank accounts. In many ways, we're powerless. What happens when we're powerless? We complain!

How can we change this dynamic?

Define what you want at your core—the *you* beneath your ego's protective layer. What gives you self-esteem? What makes you feel alive? What makes you feel loved?

Ignore money for a moment. Money is an important resource, but it has very little to do with getting to the core of what you truly want and need.

WHAT DO YOU REALLY WANT?

When was the last time you sat down and thought about what you want? I'm not talking about the daily, superficial wants that go through our heads. I'm referring to the truest desires deep down inside of us, which seldom, if ever, surface.

Initially, it might be a confusing question because we spend a lot of time, energy, and money fulfilling our wants. We want new shoes, new clothes, a new car, or a new watch. We are acting on our need for instant gratification, but we're ignoring our deeper desires that inform us of what we really want:

- To feel a positive sense of self-esteem/feel proud
- To feel a sense of belonging/feel love
- To feel excited
- To be healthy

The following is a list of our wants that, if fulfilled, lead to true meaning. I'll contrast it with what we tend to do instead—a short-term path to temporary fulfillment.

HOW TO FEEL PRIDE:

- Identify and define your core values and live a life in accordance with these values.
- Pursue goals and challenges that force you to grow as a person. The feedback loop from seeing growth is a powerful force.
- Become an independent and self-sufficient person.

THE SHORT-TERM PATH TO PRIDE:

- Buy expensive cars, houses, designer bags, and shoes to provide a temporary boost in happiness, prove our worth, and display a sense of accomplishment. This path makes us financially insecure and dependent on jobs that we may not enjoy.

HOW TO FEEL A SENSE OF BELONGING:

- Spend time with family and loved ones.
- Get involved in your local community.
- Join a club (book, sports, music, chess, etc.).
- Seek out and surround yourself with positive friends and role models.

THE SHORT-TERM PATH TO BELONGING:

- Seek approval from those that may or may not have

our best interest in mind such as bosses, certain friends, or co-workers.

- Seek out and network with people whom we perceive to have power to advance our careers or social status.
- Turn to social media, post our wins, and hope to be noticed to receive validation.

HOW TO FEEL EXCITED:

- Seek out challenges and adventures.
- Invest in experiences.
- Get involved with a hobby.

THE SHORT-TERM PATH TO EXCITEMENT:

- Buy stuff we don't need.
- Watch TV.
- Settle into a safe routine.

HOW TO BE HEALTHY:

- Eat real food as close as possible to its natural state (minimally processed).
- Don't overeat.
- Exercise three to five days a week.
- Sleep seven to nine hours each day.

- Keep a daily gratitude journal.

THERE IS NO SHORT-TERM PATH TO HEALTH.

When we feel frustrated about reaching health goals, we are tempted to:

- Eat foods that immediately please the pleasure sensors (foods high in sugar, salt, and fat).
- Succumb to short-term fad diets that don't work.
- Spend the day sitting in a chair, car, or on a couch.
- Cheat on sleep and blame it on not having enough time.
- Complain that we have so little.

Discovering your true wants is a difficult exercise. Introspection requires deep thought, work, and time. By the time we're adults, our expectations, attachments, and actions are so deeply rooted that change is hard. Not impossible, but hard. So, before we can answer this question, we need to embrace change.

THE CHANGE EQUATION

Change is something most of us need but few achieve. It requires us to admit that things aren't working and forces us out of the comfort of our familiar thoughts, beliefs, and habits. Change is disruptive and scary, but it's also necessary to be the best and most fulfilled version of you.

Change comes with two different levels: surface and underground.

Examples of surface-level changes include getting a new job, moving to a different area, changing your appearance, making new friends, or starting a hobby. These changes are important and often necessary, as they allow you to pursue new opportunities and purge toxic settings and relationships.

Underground changes include altered behaviors, tendencies, and biases. These changes have the biggest impact in removing barriers and obstacles that stop us from achieving true success, meaning, and happiness. These behaviors, tendencies, and biases tend to be buried deep inside of us and are uncomfortable to admit and reveal. Keeping them buried is often dangerous and can cause us to make unnecessary surface-level changes. In other words, we seek external changes in response to something that is really an internal problem.

So, how can one identify and change the internal issues that are holding them back? Try the change equation:

C = A + B, or Change = Accountability + Belief.

Let's isolate these variables.

ACCOUNTABILITY

To make deep changes, take ownership of what is holding you back. Accountability starts with being comfortable admitting where you are and refraining from blaming other people and/or external sources for your actions and outcomes.

Accept that they are *your* actions, and only *you* are holding yourself back.

Could your environment have shaped your outcome up to this point? Absolutely! No one should blame you for the decisions you've made. Accountability is scary because it means leaving behind the comfort of your behaviors and charting a new course. Even though the current course isn't working, it's familiar and comfortable.

BELIEF

The only way someone can take ownership and have a sense of agency is to believe that change is possible.

This is easier said than done. Belief requires confidence. How can we get the confidence needed to make change happen?

Break big goals into a series of smaller goals.

I mentioned this before, but it's worth repeating. While it is important to dream big, we need to have smaller, more achievable goals. We need short-term feedback that informs us we're on the right path. Otherwise, it's easy to get discouraged. For example, if your account balance is $0 and you set a goal to have $100,000 saved, you first need to start with a goal to save $1,000. This may mean saving $50 per paycheck. If paid twice a month, you'll meet your goal in 10 months! At that point you'll feel a sense of accomplishment, build new behaviors, and can set a new goal.

Quick side note: 69 percent of Americans have less than $1,000 saved. So, if you can get to $1,000 in the next ten months, you will have more in savings than over half of the population. Start small and make it achievable.

Seek out positive mentors or role models.

This could be a close friend, colleague, family member, celebrity, or identifying with a story about an everyday person who was able to overcome adversity. You need role models who have blazed a similar trail, truly believe in you, can encourage you, and tell you what you *need* to hear, not what you *want* to hear.

Don't let perfect be the enemy of good.

You're not perfect, and neither is the process. Every success story includes roadblocks, mistakes, and setbacks. Get comfortable with it. You're in good company.

Be easy on yourself.

Don't let tiny setbacks become bigger issues. You will make financial mistakes. I can almost guarantee it (I will too!). The key is to contain the mistake and avoid the trap of "I already messed up, so I might as well be bad." Take it easy, shake it off, and get back on track.

Change is often necessary, but hard. Don't expect change to happen overnight because change is not an event—it's a process.

$$C = A + B$$

You just need accountability and belief.

WHAT DO YOU WANT?—A GUIDE

Ready to take accountability? Do you have belief in yourself?

Good!

Let's clean the slate of expectations and ideals that have anchored, confined, and defined you up to this point. Now, back to the foundational question:

What do you want?

Given that this is such a broad and vague but important question, it's helpful to have a guide. (For your reference, I have placed this and the other accountability exercises I provide in the back of the book.) This guide is intended to organize your thoughts and identify potential roadblocks. Start by answering the following question:

How do you want to spend your time?

Imagine you were just told you have one year left to live. How would you spend your time? What would give you peace? What activities would you engage in? Who would you spend your time with? What would you want your legacy to be?

It's uncomfortable to think about death, but thinking about and accepting your own mortality is the key to living in the present. When you realize and accept that you're up against limited time (as we all are), goals, values, and important areas of your life are brought to the surface. Excess "noise" gets discarded. Thinking about your mortality is empowering, as it brings intention and urgency to your actions. By answering this question, most of your deep wants will surface.

When listing your wants, there's only one rule. They can't be material "things." Think of your deep wants as a list of the goals, places, and people you value. For each want, answer the following questions:

- What needs to happen to satisfy this want?
- Am I fulfilling any parts of this want?
- What is getting in my way (money can be included)?
- Why am I letting it get in my way?
- Are the roadblocks insurmountable? If not, how can I navigate around them?
- What will life look like if I do nothing?
- If I work toward this want, how will I feel?

WHAT NEEDS TO HAPPEN TO SATISFY THIS WANT?

Write down the decisions, actions, and steps needed

to achieve each want. It could mean reaching out and arranging time to spend with family or old friends. It could mean leaving your job and joining a new company or switching careers. Perhaps it means starting your own business or being more mindful and intentional with your money. It could mean reacquainting yourself with an old hobby or exploring something new. Don't worry about the how or when quite yet. I certainly don't expect you to leave your job tomorrow.

AM I FULFILLING ANY PARTS OF THIS WANT?

Some of these wants may be present, or partially present, in your life right now.

In this section, write down your actions, decisions, and activities fulfilling the want in the present. Write down the feelings you experience when you engage with the want. Track and write down the amount of time devoted to the want each day, week, and month. Finally, answer the question: Could I be doing more?

WHAT IS GETTING IN MY WAY (MONEY CAN BE INCLUDED)?

For each want, write down the roadblocks. Is it time, money, spouse, fear, doubt, or kids?

Basically, what is standing in your way?

WHY AM I LETTING IT?

Here's your chance to release your excuses. Act like you're venting to a friend. This should feel comforting, like you're giving yourself permission to avoid putting in the work. Embrace this feeling for just a moment because this is the last time you're allowed to use these excuses. It's for your own good.

ARE THE ROADBLOCKS INSURMOUNTABLE? IF NOT, HOW CAN I NAVIGATE AROUND THEM?

In this section, write out the steps required to work around the roadblocks. It doesn't matter how hard, difficult, or unlikely the workarounds are. Just list them out.

Want to start a business but feel you can't because of money? This is certainly a roadblock, but it's not insurmountable. In order to navigate around the lack of capital, you can:

- Create a separate savings account dedicated to reserving some seed capital. This may mean cutting expenses in another area of your life. What can you cut?

- Start the business as a side hustle while you're still working. Write a business plan, come up with a name, buy a domain, build a website, complete your legal filings, and take on a few small clients—whatever you can do on the side to move the business forward.
- Start networking. Attend conferences, tell your friends, and ask for introductions to people who may be able to help.

Will this be easy? No way! It will take discipline and intention.

Time is another excuse people love to use. We all have fifteen to seventeen hours of usable time each day. Are you working for fifteen to seventeen hours a day, seven days a week? Some weeks, maybe, but not consistently. Do you watch mindless television? Do you spend hours on social media? I'm not trying to convince you that creating more time will be easy. I am just encouraging you to believe that it's possible.

WHAT WILL LIFE LOOK LIKE IF I DO NOTHING?

If you are successful in convincing yourself that some of these wants are too hard or distant to accomplish, write down what life will be like if you don't do anything. How will you feel if you never fulfill this want? Are you OK with the outcome? The answer might be yes. That's fine.

All this means is the want is a wish. A wish that may or may not come true.

IF I WORK TOWARD THIS WANT, HOW WILL I FEEL?

Write down the feelings and emotions that come with taking the first step.

MONEY AND YOUR EGO

Defining what you want is the base of your wealth-building journey. Don't let fear, doubt, or money stop you from bringing your deep wants to the surface. Once you define your deep wants, try this exercise the next time you find yourself ready to consume. Before acting, ask yourself the following questions:

- Do I really want it?
- Is there something I want more?
- Is this going to meet one of my deeper wants?

Sounds simple enough, right? Well, it's easier said than done because defining your wants, changing your consumption patterns, and living with intention require you to confront the complicated relationship between money and your ego.

Money has become a proxy for self-worth. It's a measuring stick. It's a way to feel respected and admired. Committing to a process of financial discipline and awareness requires you to say no to things that previously informed others of your worth. Your self-esteem will no longer be tied to the brands you wear, the size of your house, the car(s) you drive, and the restaurants and clubs you frequent.

It would be a faux pas to broadcast your bank accounts, investment accounts, and paycheck. So why do we feel comfortable showing off expensive "stuff"? If your ego and self-worth are tied to how wealthy others perceive you to be, you're forced into consumption. Even if it means being financially insecure.

Think this isn't you? It may not be. But if you're in credit card debt and financially unstable, it's probably a good idea to take inventory of your "stuff" and consumption patterns. What's making you overspend? It's hard to admit, but it's probably your ego and your attachment to what your "stuff" says about your status and significance.

CHAPTER 5

Attachment

"Attachment leads to jealousy. The shadow of greed, that is. Train yourself to let go of everything you fear to lose."

—YODA

When was the last time you thought about your attachments? Have you ever? If you're like most of us, probably not. Chances are you have many attachments holding you back from being your most authentic and intentional self.

The idea of the American Dream is wrapped in attachments. We follow a specific order: high school, college, graduate school, professional career, house, kids, two vacations every year, and so on. In many ways, society created the path for us, providing a prepackaged set of expectations and outcomes. If you get the urge to break away, you better think again because the attachments have you trapped.

THINGS AND POSSESSIONS

We love our "stuff." Ask a random person to share what they would ask for if they could have anything. There's a good chance that most will have a material answer such as a car, jewelry, or a house. "Stuff" has taken the place of meaning.

We're attached to the "new" feeling. New things are fun, exciting, and exclusive. We wonder how many of our friends have something new. When we have the new thing, we get to show it off and watch as others feel tortured with the feeling of less. Sounds horrible, but we do this unconsciously. Our "things" help us define and shape our identity.

IDENTITY

We all have a need to carve out a place in this world, and we love to tell each other what that place should be. We allow others to define how our stuff—schools, jobs, cars, homes, and neighborhoods—tells us about who and what we are.

Schools and careers come in certain packages that require a similar set of actions and consumption patterns. A step up from the American Dream is the *highly-educated* American Dream, which includes college, graduate school, a corporate job, a big house in the suburbs, kids in private school, luxury cars, a country club membership, and so on. It's all part of one big predetermined package. It has to be this way for it all to make sense. Stepping outside of the walls is scary and open to criticism, disappointment, confusion, and perceived failure.

Do you want to save money and downsize the lifestyle? What will others say? Will they see you as less "successful"? Maybe. That can't happen! You've done all the "right" things. Fall in line and act accordingly. Your identity and ego demand it!

Take some time to think about your actions, your memberships, and where and how you spend your time and money. Are you doing it for you or for an identity that was decided for you?

CAREERS AND PAYCHECKS

"What do you do for a living?"

When we meet someone for the first time, there is a 99.99 percent chance that you will ask, or be asked, this question. It makes sense because our careers can say a lot about us. In theory, our careers should be the embodiment of our skills, talents, and interests. Careers allow us to quickly understand each other.

"Oh, you're a teacher!? You're probably just like my other teacher friend."

We may not say we feel this way out loud, but we certainly think it, and it's all good until we allow others to dictate our move toward or away from certain careers. It happens all the time. We "need" a certain career based on where we came from, what we think we want, and what we think we need.

But do our careers really reflect who we are as a person? For some, yes. For the masses, probably not. That said, we still attach an identity to a part of our lives that was, for many of us, unintentionally selected.

FUTURE OUTCOMES

If I do "x" and "y," then "z" will be my outcome. We see this all the time. An attachment to an outcome based on actions.

The world doesn't care about your actions, and no outcome is guaranteed. Yes, if you exercise proper diligence, work smart, and work hard, you will increase the odds of a certain outcome, but the outcome isn't guaranteed. Nothing is. Graduating from a top-rated college does not lead to automatic success. Having a professional job does not guarantee massive riches, prestige, and fulfillment. Really wanting something doesn't mean it will or should happen.

Who's to say you need a specific outcome for the effort to be successful? You may end up in a different destination but still in an amazing place.

Too often the joy of the journey gets clouded by an arbitrary, glorified outcome. By detaching actions from outcomes, you can settle in, enjoy the ride, and appreciate the ultimate destination, wherever that may be. You're not valued because of your outcomes. You are valued because you are *you*! True fulfillment does not come from achieving a particular outcome or receiving external praise. True fulfillment comes from within. It's about committing to a process, giving it your all, and knowing deep down inside you are better off for trying. The outcome is largely irrelevant. It's just a byproduct of the process and journey.

THE PAST

Everyone, including you, has the right to turn the page.

To write a new chapter that is distinct from the decisions and actions that defined your past.

Good, bad, right, or wrong, there is nothing we can do about the past. What's done is done, and every decision, action, opinion, and circumstance has led you to this point right now.

You get to decide the direction of your story. All too often we allow what defined us in the past to influence what we do in the future.

Can you relate to these statements?

- "I went to medical school; I can't leave my practice to become a writer."
- "I've neglected my finances for the last fifteen years. It's too late to open my 401(k)."
- "I had bad grades in school, so I must be dumb."

We ground ourselves based on what we did, how we were perceived, and our circumstances. We let others define our past and write our future. We stay engaged in a career, interest, or hobby because of who we used to be.

This may have all been true in the past, but your past

does not need to define who you are today. You can always chart a new course and be a new *you*!

FAIRNESS

Is it fair that billionaires exist? Is it fair that some of the wealthiest people in the world inherited their wealth? Is it fair that some people can dunk a basketball? Or paint a beautiful landscape? Or play the piano? Is it fair that some people have a genius IQ? Or a naturally thin and muscular body? If you make over $32,400 per year, is that fair? What if I told you that $32,400 puts you in the top 1 percent of income globally?[6] Would that change your perspective on fairness? The point is, we can all point to unfairness, and we can all be pointed to.

We love this attachment because it allows us to be mad, make excuses, and play the victim. Yes, unfairness exists, but you're not alone.

Give yourself one to five minutes to complain about any perceived unfairness and move on. Detach from any notion that the world should be fair. It's not.

---

6   Global Rich List, http://www.globalrichlist.com/.

ANGER

Attaching to anger is convenient. It allows us to point to someone or something else. For most of us, anger provides the permission we need to avoid the deep work. It's easy to hold onto anger, and it's hard to let go.

Attaching to anger is toxic. It doesn't change what happened, but it can, and will, influence your future actions and decisions. If you expect some closure, apology, or acknowledgment, you may be setting yourself up for disappointment because it may never come. You have no control over getting what you think you deserve, but you can choose to detach from any anger it may cause. You can address it, leave it in the past, and move forward. Did someone do you wrong? Try forgiveness. Not because they deserve forgiveness, but because you deserve peace.

ACCEPTANCE

We can't control how or what others think about us. The reality is some people will like you and some won't. It's not an indictment on you or them; it just is. Spending beyond your limits for acceptance doesn't work. Most expensive clubs, restaurants, and institutions charge what they please because they know we'll pay to be accepted. *They* know our ego needs a place at the exclusive VIP table, but *you* created the need for this acceptance.

If you're trying to keep up with an expensive crowd, you're ultimately setting yourself up for failure. Your money will eventually run out. Then what? Will you still be valued? Will you still have a positive sense of self-esteem? It's hard to admit, but there's a chance that your excess spending is for *you* to accept *yourself.*

CASE STUDY: THE ATTORNEY AND HIS PRIVATE PLANE

By all accounts Dave was rich, and at the age of fifty-eight it appeared that all of Dave's hard work had paid off. The president of a midsized law firm, Dave had $20 million in the bank, a massive house in the suburbs, a beach house, and memberships at the most exclusive clubs.

Yet, Dave was miserable. He was out of shape, sleep-deprived, and unfulfilled. The life of a corporate attorney, filled with long hours, travel, and demanding clients, was killing him. His role caused him to be short-tempered, unreasonable, and just plain mean. He did not like the person he had become.

At one of our quarterly review meetings, Dave went

on about how much he hated being an attorney and how he longed to spend more time traveling to watch his son play college tennis. He had missed most of his son's high school matches and feared college would also slip away.

The solution to his issues appeared to be clear. He could quit his job, retire, travel, and live on his $20 million. But there was a problem. He didn't have enough for a private plane. He went on to explain that his successful friends and clients—CEOs and founders of multibillion-dollar companies—had private planes. To him, that was the standard of success, and without it, there was no way he would be professionally fulfilled and accepted as a peer. He was adamant that chartered flights or private aviation membership plans wouldn't cut it. In his view, he wouldn't be able to retire until he had at least $100 million saved. So, he went on with his life. Dave was unhappy and time constrained all because he was attached to the idea that a private plane was the definition of success. He was trapped. This attachment owned his life, and it was all an illusion.

I know what you're thinking. "This guy is ridiculous!" You're right, but to him it wasn't ridiculous. This was his reality, and he was benchmarking himself and his success based on his closest peers. Do you do this as well? Do you have any attachments solely based on your own microreality? Do you have attachments that probably seem ridiculous to a casual outside observer? My guess is yes.

ATTACHMENT AND BUDDHISM

"Attachment is the source of all suffering."

—BUDDHA

Buddhism is a philosophy of joy, meaning, and connection. In many ways, it's the exact opposite of mindless consumerism and competition. But joy, meaning, and connection can only be achieved through an understanding and acceptance of suffering. Attachment (or nonattachment) is the bridge between suffering and enlightenment.

Suffering is hard to understand. Why does it happen? Where does it come from? Why are some given small doses, and others large? Why do natural disasters occur? These questions are impossible to answer, because suffering just happens. It's part of the human condition, and herein lies the problem of our perception and understanding of suffering. Our attachments are born out of our need to explain and control the world around us. They help us feel secure and act as walls to protect us from suffering's truth and be exempt from suffering's wrath. Of course, we're not exempt, and understanding and accepting this truth is the key to ending our suffering. Instead of operating in isolation in the world around us, we can act in concert. Our attachments are just an illusion, and when we let go, joy, power, self-acceptance, and freedom await us.

THE DETACHMENT FRAMEWORK

There is a way to detach that doesn't involve joining a monastery. You can reclaim control over your self-esteem and self-worth. It all starts with stepping outside of yourself.

STEP 1

Write a description of the main character in a book, TV show, or movie that you most admire. Next, answer the following questions:

- Who are they (write their bio)?
- What are their strengths?
- What are their weaknesses?
- What makes them special?
- What are their flaws?
- Why do you respect them?

- How do their material things or possessions influence the way you think about them?
- What attracts you to them?
- What are their attachments, and how are they a disservice to the person's character?

By going through this exercise, you'll hopefully notice that your admiration has nothing to do with stuff, careers, or money. What attracts us to these characters are their vulnerabilities, courage, convictions, expertise, integrity, and soulfulness.

Do you think James Bond is admired because of the gadgets, cars, and models? Sure, these additions are awesome, but that's not what we admire. We admire his confidence, courage, and the unwavering belief he has in himself, even in the darkest of times.

Do people love Elle Woods because of her wealth, cars, and clothes? Yes, her character is always stylish and well put together, but that's not what we admire. We admire her strength, resiliency, intelligence, and her willingness to stand up for herself and others.

STEP 2

Repeat this same process, but for a character you most

despise such as a villain, nemesis, or cheater. Answer the following questions:

- Who are they (write their bio)?
- What are their strengths?
- What are their weaknesses?
- What are their flaws?
- How do their material things or possessions influence the way you think about them?
- What do you find unattractive about them?
- Next, write out their attachments (don't feel constrained to the examples highlighted above).

Think of Mr. Potter in the movie *It's a Wonderful Life*. He was the wealthiest man in town, but he was lonely, mean, and attached to his identity as a powerful and successful banker. He led through fear and intimidation. He was a miserable and hated character. Yet we love George Bailey—the broke, depressed, and flawed hero. See where I'm going here?

STEP 3

Repeat this process for yourself. Answer these questions:

- Who are you (write your bio)?

- What are your strengths?
- What are your weaknesses?
- What are your flaws?
- What roles do material things play in your life?
- What are your attachments, and how are they holding you back?

STEP 4

Repeat this process, but this time, for the Future You. The detached version of you. Please note that this version will not be perfect, and that's the point. This version of you is detached from the idea of perfection. There is great wealth outside the walls of our attachments. Wealth that is waiting to be claimed.

CHAPTER 6

Defining Wealth on Your Terms

"It's good to have money and the things that money can buy, but it's good, too, to check up once in a while and make sure that you haven't lost the things that money can't buy."

—GEORGE HORACE LORIMER

Wealth is a broad term, and its meaning and interpretation can take on many forms. We tend to associate wealth with money and "things." We allow other people, institutions, and popular culture to define wealth—it's meaning and associated prestige and power.

While money is important, it's just one component of wealth. Like goals, expectations, and personal benchmarks, wealth can be defined on your own terms. There are so many valuable and important areas of your life, including time, love, knowledge, adventure, and health. They are all components of wealth, and you have the capacity for true abundance.

TIME

Who would you rather be: an eighty-two-year-old billionaire or a twenty-two-year-old with an unwritten future? I assume the latter. What does this tell you? Time is so much more valuable than money. You can always make more money, but you can't make more time.

We can't stop or reverse time, but we can be more intentional about how we spend our moments. If not, we allow time to pass without acting on the experiences and challenges that provide meaning and purpose.

You will never get this moment back, and tomorrow will come too quickly if you don't stop and embrace all that is happening right now. Having a bad day and can't wait for tomorrow? Well, guess what? Tomorrow will also bring challenges, setbacks, and worries. The solution to your problem isn't tomorrow; the solution is to get reacquainted with today.

UNCONDITIONAL LOVE

Nothing can make you feel wealth and abundance like being surrounded by those you love—those who really know you. They are the ones who respect your strengths and vulnerabilities. They love you unconditionally. Unconditional love has nothing to do with money. You can't buy true love, and trying to control others with money and expecting unconditional love doesn't work. Instead, it's about how we make each other feel. It's about showing your support, listening, and allowing your loved ones to struggle while being their biggest cheerleader. All of this is free. It just comes down to spending time with friends and loved ones, caring about others, and allowing others to care for you.

KNOWLEDGE

"(S)he is a wealth of knowledge." We've heard this before: an abundance of knowledge being referred to as a "wealth" of knowledge. Knowledge is power. It can't be taken from you; it's transferrable and valuable.

We hear stories of people having their money stripped away due to bad investments, businesses and industries going out of business, and relatives stealing from beneficiaries. People can steal your money and/or take away your income, but they can't steal knowledge. Has a family member stolen something from you? Well, if you have knowledge, you can rebuild.

Knowledge comes in two forms: a hunger for learning and experience. Today, learning is more accessible and inexpensive than ever before (excluding higher education). All it takes is a commitment to learn. Read books and watch documentaries. Listen to TED Talks and browse YouTube. Knowledge is there for the taking. Experience and wisdom come with living life with your eyes, ears, and heart wide open.

ADVENTURE

Adventures make us feel alive, challenges our status quo, and helps us explore the depths of our capabilities. Think about your last adventure. How did it make you feel? Did it challenge you or make you feel alive?

Who has more abundance in their life: the person who made a lot of money by working a hundred weeks rotting under florescent lights, or the person who saw the world, took risks, and experienced different jobs, customs, and cultures? There is great wealth behind our adventures. Wealth that has no price tag.

HEALTH

Material things hold little value if your health is in serious decline. Our minds and bodies are our most precious resource. Health must be celebrated and protected, but as a society, we're health-poor:

- Two-thirds of Americans are overweight.[7]
- Over 30 percent of adults are considered obese.[8]
- Heart disease is the leading cause of death for both men and women in the US (647,000 per year!).[9]

Treat your body the way you would treat something or someone that is important to you. If you live by this mantra, you will think twice before smoking that cigarette, eating that doughnut, abusing alcohol, working endless hours at a meaningless job, or sitting on the couch for hours on end. This is an area of your life where it pays to be greedy. We should all strive for the greatest wealth of health.

---

7 "Obesity and Overweight," National Center for Health Statistics, Centers for Disease Control and Prevention, June 13, 2016, https://www.cdc.gov/nchs/fastats/obesity-overweight.htm.

8 "Obesity and Overweight," https://www.cdc.gov/nchs/fastats/obesity-overweight.htm.

9 "Heart Disease Facts," Centers for Disease Control and Prevention, December 2, 2019, https://www.cdc.gov/heartdisease/facts.htm.

Joe teaches eighth-grade math at a suburban public school. He makes $60,000 annually, and after taxes, retirement/pension contributions, and insurance, nets $2,800 each month. He is married with two kids and lives in a modest three-bedroom, two-bathroom house about an hour from work. Joe's wife, Katie, is also a teacher, and, like Joe, nets $2,800 each month. In addition, they earn a combined $833 monthly in coaching and side hustle income.

When Joe and Katie got married, they decided to have a small and affordable wedding, and put their "wedding savings" and cash gifts towards a down payment on a $250,000 house. Today, their monthly housing expenses (mortgage, maintenance, and taxes) are $1,500. Joe and Katie each went to local universities and have zero student loan debt.

Each month, childcare expenses are $1,000 (after school activities), and food, household (gas, car insurance, utilities, phone), and entertainment expenses total $2,000. Unexpected monthly expenses do come up from time to time and average around $200. They drive modest cars that are paid off in full, rarely go out to eat, and are mindful about every expense. Finally, they attempt to contribute at least $1,000 each month to their various savings and investment accounts.

Here's an at-a-glance view of their financial picture:

JOE AND KATIE

ANNUAL AFTER-TAX INCOME	
Joe's After-Tax (and retirement contribution) Income	$33,600
Katie's After-Tax (and retirement contribution) Income	$33,600
Camp and Coaching Income	$10,000
TOTAL ANNUAL TAKE HOME INCOME	**$77,200**

EXPENSES AND SAVINGS	
Mortgage, Home Maintenance, and Taxes	$18,000
Child Care (Camp and After School Activities)	$12,000
Food, Household Expenses, Entertainment Expenses	$24,000
Miscellaneous Expenses	$2,400
Vacation Savings Fund	$6,000
Investment and Savings Accounts	$14,800
TOTAL EXPENSES AND SAVINGS	**$77,200**

The entire family is active and engaged in sports. Joe loves soccer and takes part whenever he can. He plays in a weekly league, coaches his son's weekend team, is an assistant coach for the eighth-grade team, and is an instructor at a local four-week summer soccer camp.

Joe loves being healthy and connected to his favorite sport.

Katie is an avid runner and coaches the school's cross-country team. She is a member of the local running club and typically runs four races a year, including a marathon. The kids are also active and engaged in sports. Joe and Katie live close to their respective families and spend most Sundays at a family member's house.

Each summer the family takes a weeklong vacation to a local beach destination and they use long weekends for quick getaway trips. Life is busy, and full of abundance.

Joe and Katie are not cash rich. They don't drive luxury cars, live in a fancy house, go to expensive restaurants, or take luxury vacations. Yet, they receive great joy, purpose, and value from their jobs as educators, their activities, and, most of all, spending time with loved ones. Joe and Katie are wealthy.

CASE STUDY: JOHN, THE POOR INVESTMENT BANKER

John is a managing director at a big-city investment bank. He makes $2 million annually and after taxes, insurance, and retirement contributions nets approximately $100,000 each month.

John and his wife, Lisa, live in their 7,000-square-foot dream house with six bedrooms, seven bathrooms, a gym, a chef's kitchen, and a swimming pool in an exclusive suburban community. Their three kids go to an elite private school, and they belong to a local country club, beach club, and golf club. They take three vacations each year (one week for spring break, two weeks over the summer, and one week over the holidays). They drive luxury cars, wear designer clothes, drink expensive wine, and have expensive hobbies. Given their lifestyle, expenses add up fast.

Here's a snapshot of their financial picture:

ANNUAL AFTER-TAX INCOME	
John's After-Tax (and retirement contribution) Income	$1,200,000
TOTAL ANNUAL TAKE HOME INCOME	**$1,200,000**

EXPENSES AND SAVINGS	
Mortgage, Home Maintenance, and Taxes	$300,000
Private School Tuition	$150,000
Club Dues	$100,000
Vacations	$100,000
Clothes, Watches, Jewelry, Wine	$60,000
Private Coaches, Tutors, Camps	$40,000
Food and Entertainment	$80,000
New Car	$80,000
Other Miscellaneous Expenses	$60,000
Investment and Savings Accounts	$230,000
TOTAL EXPENSES AND SAVINGS	**$1,200,000**

Even though expenses are high, $230,000 is still a lot in savings. But what happens if a recession hits? What if John's compensation declines? What if he loses his job? Is this enough of a buffer to sustain the family's lifestyle during a difficult time? To make matters worse, John is miserable.

The seventy-plus-hour workweeks are taking a toll on

his health and well-being. At the age of forty-six, he is eighty pounds overweight and on a steady diet of prescription meds. His work has forced him to leave vacations early, cancel dinner plans, miss school plays, sports events, and recitals. He feels like he's missing his kids grow up, and that he and Lisa have lost touch. They rarely spend time together, have little to talk about, and are under chronic stress and pressure.

Life wasn't supposed to be this way. John and Lisa were both great students and always wanted the "good life" for their family. John never set out to be an investment banker, but it seemed like the right thing to do and he thought money would solve all issues. John and Lisa are income and cash wealthy but broke everywhere else.

CASE STUDY: ASHLEY, THE POOR TEACHER

Ashley is a middle school teacher in an affluent suburb. Her annual salary is $60,000, and after taxes, retirement and pension contributions, and insurance, she nets $2,800 each month. Ashley's husband, Rob, is also a teacher and, like Ashley, nets $2,800 each month.

Ashley and Rob were married last year, and their parents offered to contribute $20,000 to their wedding fund. While grateful, they wanted a dream wedding and spent an extra $15,000. They paid for the overage with a credit card. Today, their credit card balance is still $15,000 at an interest rate of 20 percent ($3,000 per year). In addition, despite receiving a partial scholarship to the local state university, Ashley decided to go to an out-of-state private college and has $40,000 in student loans, costing $500 per month.

Ashley and Rob live in a trendy neighborhood and pay $2,200 in monthly rent. They both lease new cars that cost (including insurance) $500 per month ($1,000 total). They rarely cook at home, and their monthly food and entertainment expenses are roughly $2,000. Finally, miscellaneous expenses and subscription services come in around $600 each month. If you're doing the math, things don't look good.

Let's look at their finances:

ANNUAL AFTER-TAX INCOME

Ashley's After-Tax (and retirement contribution) Income	$33,600
Rob's After-Tax (and retirement contribution) Income	$33,600
TOTAL ANNUAL TAKE HOME INCOME	**$67,200**

EXPENSES AND SAVINGS

Rent	$26,400
Student Loans	$6,000
Car Payments	$12,000
Food, Household Expenses, Entertainment Expenses	$24,000
Miscellaneous Expenses	$7,200
Credit Card Interest	$3,000
TOTAL EXPENSES AND SAVINGS	**$78,600**

Throw in two vacations each year, and their credit card balance and interest payments are only going up. To make matters worse, they live a sedentary lifestyle, and the lack of activity combined with takeout food has resulted in weight gain, unhealthy habits, and a toxic mindset.

Each night, they settle in to watch reality TV, and it's a constant reminder of what they don't have. This makes them angry, resentful, and unhappy with their day-to-day lives. Everyone else seems to have so much more!

Ashley and Rob are in major debt when it comes to their wealth, health, and overall state of being. Ashley and Rob are poor.

CASE STUDY: LORI, THE WEALTHY INVESTMENT BANKER

Lori is an investment banker at a large, big-city bank. She lives in the heart of the city and loves the urban lifestyle. Lori's husband, Mike, works part-time as a consultant. They have two young children, and Mike takes on the lion's share of the day-to-day childcare duties.

Lori loves her job. She always wanted to work on Wall Street and feeds off the excitement and energy of the deal-making process. Lori makes $2 million annually and after taxes, insurance, and retirement contributions, nets approximately $100,000 each month. Mike makes an additional $11,000 annually (after taxes) in consulting income. He views his work as more of a hobby to keep him intellectually engaged.

They have a high income, but life in the big city can be expensive. Let's look at what they bring in and what goes out:

ANNUAL AFTER-TAX INCOME

Lori's After-Tax (and retirement contribution) Income	$1,200,000
Mike's After-Tax (and retirement contribution) Income	$11,000
TOTAL ANNUAL TAKE HOME INCOME	**$1,211,000**

EXPENSES AND SAVINGS

Rent	$100,000
Clothes, Watches, Jewelry	$6,000
Vacations	$30,000
Food, Household Expenses, Entertainment Expenses	$40,000
Private Coaches, Tutors, Camps	$20,000
Miscellaneous Expenses	$15,000
Investment and Savings Accounts	$1,000,000
TOTAL EXPENSES AND SAVINGS	**$1,211,000**

Lori and Mike enjoy their careers, make a good living, and live in a safe and comfortable neighborhood. Yes, their apartment is expensive, but they can afford it, and the location allows Lori to spend less time commuting and more time at home.

Lori and Mike indulge on travel, activities for their kids, and entertainment, but they are also saving a high percentage of their after-tax income. Lori knows she can't be an investment banker forever and will eventually want (and need) to slow down. By being intentional, Lori and Mike control life events on their terms. They have the same income as John and Lisa, but a much different outcome. Lori and Mike are wealthy.

CAN SOMEONE REALLY LIVE ON A BUDGET OF $1 MILLION PER YEAR?

Newly divorced with a young daughter, Natalie's life was in a state of disarray. For the previous nine years, she was the proud wife of an up-and-coming New York City hedge fund manager. She wasn't from money but quickly got used to the socialite lifestyle. Days were spent shopping, attending fancy lunches, and being part of the scene. Having a child didn't change much. With a full-time nanny, her life was business as usual.

Suddenly, everything changed. Her husband wanted a divorce. He was in love with a younger woman. After a short legal battle, Natalie walked away with $5 million and child/spousal support of $1 million per year for the next nine years. She was panicked and scared. At our introductory meeting, the first words out of her mouth were:

"Can someone really live on a budget of $1 million per year?!"

This may sound crazy, but this was the life she had grown accustomed to. It was her new normal, and it was being disrupted. When talking about the divorce, she acknowledged that she had been unhappy for years. The lifestyle was not providing joy or meaning, but it was comfortable and familiar. One million dollars is a lot of money, but it wasn't enough to keep up with the lifestyle that nonetheless left her unhappy and unfulfilled. In many ways, she was poor.

WEALTH ON *YOUR* TERMS

Money is important, but only so long as it allows you the flexibility and time to pursue the areas of great purpose. At the end of the day, it all comes down to trading time for money. We need to spend time to acquire money, but once we have enough to satisfy our basic needs, every extra minute spent working at a meaningless job to chase more money creates a deficit in another important area of your life.

Spending is also a crucial part of the equation because unintentional spending uses up our cash resources and forces us back to work in order to live. When this dynamic occurs, we are a slave to our stuff. It's a vicious cycle. Stuff-rich, but poor in all other areas. We become the victim of our own doing.

Are you trading your money (and time) for something that is truly valuable to *you*? We all have the power to be wealthy. It comes down to identifying and creating abundance in every important area of *your* life.

"The real measure of your wealth is how much you'd be worth if you lost all your money."

—UNKNOWN

CHAPTER 7

It's Not About What You Want

"All our dreams can come true, if we have the courage to pursue them."

—WALT DISNEY

Are you inspired? Do you feel a sense of clarity? I hope so.

We love inspiration. Inspiration gives us hope. It provides support and encouragement in the darkest of times, but inspiration doesn't *do* anything. Inspiration doesn't write books, create art, take you the distance of a marathon, lose weight, or build wealth. Inspiration is just an emotion. Like happiness, sadness, fear, greed, jealousy, or pride, inspiration is something we feel. Like most feelings and emotions, inspiration is fleeting. Here one moment and gone the next. When inspiration goes away, you move on to the next emotion; you return to your comfortable ways.

Creating change, making a difference, and seeing progress toward your goals and wants is not about finding inspiration. Writing down what you want is just the start, and really wanting something doesn't turn it into a reality. Commitment does. It's not about what you want; it's about what you're willing to commit to. It's about taking action.

NEW YEAR'S RESOLUTIONS (FAILS)

> "I want to be healthy, lose weight, feel fit, eat better, cook more, run a marathon, and save more money."

These are all common New Year's resolutions, but chances are none of these wants will be accomplished. It's estimated that 80 percent of New Year's resolutions fail by mid-February.

Why do so many genuine wants fail to become reality? It's not due to lack of desire or sincerity. Most people really do want to accomplish their stated goals. It's because we only wish for the outcome and fail to accept the cruel reality that accomplishing these goals will take dedication and a lot of hard work. Conquering anything great requires commitment and a willingness to show up. So, how can we put our goals into action? Use the following commitment framework:

WHAT DO I WANT?

- I want to build wealth.

WHAT AM I WILLING TO COMMIT TO?

- Take the time to organize my bills and accounts.
- Track expenses at the end of each day.
- Create and manage a budget.
- Learn how to invest and open an investment account by the end of the month.
- Pay myself first.
- Increase my 401(k) contribution up to the employer match.

Create your own list of what you're willing to commit to, revisit your commitments at least once per month, and hold yourself accountable.

BE SPECIFIC AND REALISTIC

As you can see, there is a big difference between

saying what you want and committing to a specific set of actions. Be specific and realistic with your commitments and start small to build good habits. All positive results start with a goal but become a reality by committing to a consistent process.

JUST START

Starting is scary. It takes guts. Starting something new forces you to embrace your vulnerabilities and the unknown. When you start something new, you're not very good. This leaves you exposed to criticism (mostly self-inflicted) and embarrassment. But we need to be starters because the only way we can be the best version of ourselves is to explore and push the limits of our perceived capabilities. So, how can you push past the mental barriers and get started? Use the strategies that follow to spark and fan your flame.

EMBRACE YOUR VULNERABILITIES

Vulnerability is our greatest asset. When you embrace your vulnerabilities, you take the greatest leaps in terms of personal growth. Just look at children.

When kids learn to walk, they stumble and fall after just a couple of steps. Yet, they pick themselves up and keep trying. Falling more along the way. They learn to talk by making sounds, but then sounds become words, and words become sentences. Kids experience spurts of personal growth by bringing their vulnerabilities to the surface and accepting help and guidance along the way. They have no choice.

Adults have a choice, and most of us choose to mask our vulnerabilities. We hide from our deficiencies, resist help, and prioritize comfort over personal growth. This is especially true when it comes to money.

SET THE BENCHMARK

The most exciting part about starting something new is the ability to set the benchmark. When you start, set the benchmark as low as possible. If you start from the couch and say you're going to be a runner, your benchmark is just getting off the couch. Next, you reset the benchmark by running a half mile. Then, you run for one mile. Then, two miles and so on. If you start with nothing in savings, your benchmark is putting $1 in a savings account. Then you reset the benchmark by saving $100. Then save $500. Next, save $1,000. The best part about benchmarking is *you* get to establish the threshold. All you need to worry about is beating who you were last week, month, and year.

BE PROUD

Make no mistake about it: starting is hard. It requires strength and courage. A successful start is defined by developing the right habits to ensure continued success over the long term, not by how quickly you accomplish your goal. When you open a savings account and contribute the first $100, you should feel pride. Why? Because you had the guts to start. Building wealth requires deliberate action because wants and hopes are not a plan.

Part 3

You Can Take Action

CHAPTER 8

Money As a Resource

"Money isn't the most important thing in life, but it's reasonably close to oxygen on the 'gotta have it' scale."

—ZIG ZIGLAR

Clean water is a precious resource. In the Western world, clean water is in abundance, and it feels like it always will be. But what if there was no implicit water guarantee? Would you treat your water consumption differently? Would you store water for the future? Would you be a little scared?

Absolutely!

If we feel this way about a natural resource, shouldn't we apply the same rules and logic to money?

Money is a resource. To be clear, a scarce resource. We need money to buy day-to-day necessities such as food, shelter, clothing, and transportation. Money is a tool for survival. Next to oxygen, water, and our bodies, money is our most important resource. We trade our time, freedom, and labor in exchange for it.

When we're young, we tend to take money for granted. We assume paychecks will keep coming and that our money faucet will never dry up. The idea that there will come a day when we will no longer have access to earning more of this resource is easy to ignore. It might seem fun to consume now and ignore the future, but that mindset leads to peril. There will come a day when you will experience scarcity of this once abundant resource. It may come sooner than you think. Saving for the future is not just about some abstract retirement. It's about having a safety net for the next recession, or saving for that dream vacation or a down payment on your forever home. Saving is about being financially independent so you don't have to wait forty years to control your time.

Respecting your wealth requires deliberate action. Define and quantify your goals. Establish a budget and savings plan that's aligned with your goals and values. Invest your excess reserves to keep your money working, even when you're not. There is power that comes with conserving and investing this precious resource.

CHAPTER 9

Where Are You?

"Start where you are. Use what you have. Do what you can."

—ARTHUR ASHE

Think back to your last journey. Did you travel overseas? Maybe you went back to school or lost thirty pounds.

Did any of those things just happen because you wanted them to happen?

No!

Things happen because you decide to take the journey. All journeys take intention, patience, and organization.

Building wealth is no different. We need a destination and directions to get there. First, we need to know where to start.

FINANCIAL NET WORTH STATEMENT (YOUR WEALTH COORDINATES)

Most of us have no clue what we hold in assets, how much we owe in debt, when bills need to be paid, or what it means to pay interest. This "head in the sand" approach keeps us stuck in a state of financial pain and misery.

Before we can move forward and start the wealth-building process, we need a picture of where things currently stand—the good, the bad, and the ugly. The financial practitioner's term for this document is a net worth statement.

A net worth statement takes the value of your assets (checking accounts, savings accounts, investment accounts, retirement accounts, home value, etc.) and subtracts your debts (credit card debt, mortgage debt, personal loans, etc.).

The result is the amount left over if your assets were liquidated (sold and turned into cash), and all debts paid off in full. You can think of your financial net worth statement as a measure of your financial health.

Your net worth statement is fluid and needs to be updated on a monthly basis so you can see progress, confront regressions, and remain on track toward your financial goals. Most importantly, updating your net worth statement on a monthly basis tells you where you are, not where you think you are or where you want to be.

For those with significant wealth, this is a fun exercise. You get to see your wealth staring back at you. For those in the middle of the wealth-building journey, this is an exciting exercise. You get to see your progress on paper. For those starting the wealth-building process (or thinking of starting), this exercise is terrifying. It exposes past mistakes and reveals the long road ahead. But you need to confront and accept your current financial positioning because all progress starts with seeing yourself exposed and committing to change.

HOW TO ORGANIZE

STEP 1: LIST YOUR ASSETS WITH THEIR CORRESPONDING VALUES:

- All checking accounts
- All savings accounts—List an associated goal with each one such as general savings, emergency savings, down payment fund, etc.
- All investment accounts—Label each one: retirement, 401(k), general investment account, etc.

- Real estate—Use a service like Zillow to get a sense of your property's value, but it's best to just value at either cost, based on sales of similar homes in your area, or get a professional appraisal.
- Private business interests—List at cost, based on values of similar companies, or any recent professional valuation.

STEP 2: LIST YOUR DEBTS (LIABILITIES):

- List all credit cards, mortgage payments, student loans, and personal loans.

STEP 3: SUBTRACT THE SUM OF YOUR LIABILITIES (DEBTS) FROM THE SUM OF YOUR ASSETS.

This is your financial net worth. Update this document on a monthly basis and track your progress.

Here is a template for your reference:

Future You Wealth
Save, Invest, And Spend With Intention

YOUR NAME

FINANCIAL NET WORTH STATEMENT

DATE

ASSETS

BANK XYZ CHECKING ACCOUNT	$5,232
EMERGENCY SAVINGS ACCOUNT	$30,000
VACATION SAVINGS ACCOUNT	$1,500
INVESTMENT ACCOUNT	$11,572
401(K)	$65,323
ROTH IRA	$14,652
HOUSE ESTIMATE	$300,000
CAR ESTIMATE	$10,000
TOTAL	**$438,279**

LIABILITIES

XYZ CREDIT CARD RECENT STATEMENT BALANCE (TO BE PAID OFF IN FULL)	$1,873
XYZ CREDIT CARD RECURRING BALANCE	$0
CAR LOAN BALANCE	$11,720
MORTGAGE	$240,000
STUDENT LOAN BALANCE	$27,252
TOTAL	**$280,845**

NET WORTH (ASSETS-LIABILITIES)	**$157,434**

CHAPTER 10

Where Are You Going?

Alice: "Would you tell me, please, which way I ought to go from here?"

Cheshire Cat: "That depends a good deal on where you want to get to,"

Alice: "I don't much care where—"

Cheshire Cat: "Then it doesn't matter which way you go,"

Alice: "—so long as I get somewhere,"

Cheshire Cat: "Oh, you're sure to do that, if you only walk long enough."[10]

—LEWIS CARROLL, *ALICE'S ADVENTURES IN WONDERLAND*

---

10   Patricia Elzie-Tuttle, "36 of My Favorite *Alice in Wonderland* Quotes," BookRiot, November 24, 2017, https://bookriot.com/2017/11/24/alice-in-wonderland-quotes/.

To get to where you want to go, you must know where you're going. When it comes to building wealth, goals are your destination.

DEFINING GOALS AND OBJECTIVES

Define wealth goals that are aligned with your true wants, values, and desires. Divide your goals into three categories: short, intermediate, and long-term.

SHORT-TERM GOALS:

These are goals like paying off debt, establishing an emergency savings fund, or saving for a vacation, experience, or saving for your child's college—anything you want to accomplish within the next year or two.

INTERMEDIATE-TERM GOALS:

These types of goals take longer, such as buying a home, traveling the world for a year, or starting a business—anything you want to accomplish in the next three to ten years.

LONG-TERM GOALS:

These are goals you want to accomplish in more than ten years, such as saving for your retirement.

The timing of these goals is unique to *you*. Your retirement goal may be five years away, and that's fine. The categorized goals I provided are just a guide.

Accept that goals will change over time. Life happens. People and values change. By starting the process today, you will develop the right behaviors and habits that will allow you to make any needed adjustments.

QUANTIFYING GOALS AND OBJECTIONS

How much should you be saving toward each goal?

SHORT-TERM GOALS:

These are the easiest to quantify, and there is an order of operations. Pay off credit card debt first. Then, start an emergency savings. Finally, tackle all other short-term savings goals last.

Paying off credit card debt

Credit card debt must be paid off as quickly as possible.

If you have $5,000 in credit card debt, pick an end date (try to make it within twelve months) and save a set amount each month to meet the deadline. Do you want to pay off your balances in ten months? Can you carve out $500 from your current expenses (eat at home more often, say no to new clothes, and ditch the lattes)? If so, set the intention to pay off $500 of the debt each month. Interest will accrue along the way, so it will take a little longer than ten months, but by setting the goal and charting the course, in ten months you will be in striking distance of being credit card debt free! Credit card debt is expensive. A balance of $5,000 will cost you around $1,000 in interest each year, and $1,000 can be put to better use. You will never regret paying off your credit card debt. Make this goal a priority.

Establishing an emergency savings fund

After paying off credit card debt, it's time to establish an emergency savings fund. An appropriate target is six months of living expenses. I call this my "power fund"! Unwanted life events happen without advanced notice. Cars break down, companies cut jobs, and pets get sick. You can't control negative events that happen around you, but you can be prepared. An emergency savings fund allows you to respond to life's negative surprises from a position of power.

Other short-term savings goals

After paying off credit card debt and establishing an emergency savings fund, work on saving for fun things and experiences that are aligned with your values like a vacation, a side hustle fund, new furniture, or a new car.

INTERMEDIATE-TERM GOALS

The biggest difference between short-term and intermediate-term goals is that you can work on multiple intermediate-term goals concurrently.

Buying a home

If you're buying a home, you'll need a down payment that represents 20 percent of the home's value. Yes, there are financing options that require less, but let's use 20 percent as a baseline. Owning a home is expensive, and if you can't comfortably afford a 20 percent down payment, you may want to reconsider buying the home. If you want to buy a home valued at $300,000, you'll need a down payment of $60,000. Segregate these funds in a separate account, not in your emergency savings fund. Start this goal after you pay off credit card debt and reach your emergency savings target, but concurrently with other short, intermediate, and long-term goals.

Saving for college

Do you have young children, and do you want to pay for their higher education expenses? Start saving now through a 529 plan. A 529 plan is a tax-free education savings fund that provides exposure to various investments, including the stock market. How much will you need? It all depends on the age of your child and what college they plan to attend. Here is a great resource to help you quantify how much you'll need in the future, and how much to set aside today: https://www.savingforcollege.com/.

LONG-TERM GOALS

For most of us, our primary long-term saving goal is retirement. Even if you think you'll never actually retire, this is still an important goal.

Retirement may be hard to envision now, but there's a good chance a day will come when you will want to slow down, do more meaningful work, or have more control over your time. Regardless of how you define or envision retirement, a healthy financial foundation is critical to supporting your desired lifestyle. Trust that you will not regret making this a priority. Your future self will thank you.

How much will you need for retirement?

It all comes down to four variables—your spending, timing, starting value, and monthly/annual contributions.

Step 1: *Estimate how much you will spend annually in retirement.*

It's next to impossible to know what your expenses will look like in retirement, so just use your current annual expenses. For this example, let's assume you spend $80,000 per year.

Step 2: *Determine what an annual spend of $80,000 will be equivalent to at your desired retirement age.*

What does this mean? Well, there is a silent threat to your savings and future spending called inflation. Inflation is the force that makes goods, commodities, and services more expensive in the future compared to their prices today. Inflation is the reason movie tickets no longer cost a nickel. So, what does $80,000 look like forty years into the future? If you assume an inflation rate of 2.5 percent, the calculation is as follows: $80,000 x (1.025^40) = $215,000. In other words, in forty years, annual spending of $215,000 will be equivalent to spending $80,000 today.

Step 3: *Calculate how much you will need in forty years to support $215,000 of annual expenses.*

A quick and easy way is to multiply your estimated future expenses by 25: $215,000 x 25 = $5,375,000.

Step 4: *Calculate how much you will need to save and invest each month to meet this goal.*

Here is a useful calculator: https://www.msn.com/en-us/money/tools/timevalueofmoney. Go to the monthly payment tab, enter $5,375,000 in future value, $0 in present value, 8 percent annual interest, compound monthly, and forty years. In the output, you will see that you need to save and invest $1,540 each month.

Sounds like a lot, but your 401(k) is a great savings vehicle to use for the bulk of your retirement savings. If your company offers a contribution match, your savings goal becomes even easier. And, of course, the less you spend, the less you need. If you can live off $30,000 (in today's dollars) and want to retire in ten years, you'll need $960,000. If you start with $0 today, you'll need to save and invest $5,247 each month.

For easy reference, refer to the following tables: How Much Will I Need for Retirement? and How Much Do I Need to Contribute Each Month?

How Much Will I Need for Retirement?

Using the "How Much Will I Need for Retirement?" table, estimate your annual retirement expenses (in today's dollars), and select the number of years until retirement. Where the two meet is your retirement savings goal. For example, if you anticipate annual spending of $50,000 (in today's dollars) and plan on retiring in forty years, your retirement savings target is around $3.3 million. This assumes an inflation rate of 2.5 percent and annual investment returns of 8 percent (.67 percent each month).

FUTURE YOU WEALTH
SAVE, INVEST, AND SPEND WITH INTENTION

RETIREMENT SAVINGS GOAL

	$200,000	$6,400,423	$8,193,082	$10,487,838	$13,425,319	$17,185,544
	$175,000	$5,600,370	$7,168,947	$9,176,858	$11,747,154	$15,037,351
	$150,000	$4,800,317	$6,144,812	$7,865,878	$10,068,989	$12,889,158
	$125,000	$4,000,264	$5,120,676	$6,554,899	$8,390,824	$10,740,965
	$100,000	$3,200,211	$4,096,541	$5,243,919	$6,712,660	$8,592,772
	$75,000	$2,400,159	$3,072,406	$3,932,939	$5,034,495	$6,444,579
	$50,000	$1,600,106	$2,048,271	$2,621,959	$3,356,330	$4,296,386
	$25,000	$800,053	$1,024,135	$1,310,980	$1,678,165	$2,148,193
		10	20	30	40	50

ANNUAL EXPENSES (TODAY'S DOLLARS)

YEARS TO RETIREMENT (THE DATE WHEN YOU WILL STOP WORKING)

Using the "How Much Do I Need to Contribute Each Month?" table, estimate your annual retirement expenses (in today's dollars), and select the number of years until retirement. Where the two meet is your monthly contribution goal (same inflation and return assumptions as above). For example, if you anticipate annual spending of $50,000 (in today's dollars) and plan to retire in forty years, you'll need to contribute and invest around $960 each month.

FUTURE YOU WEALTH
SAVE, INVEST, AND SPEND WITH INTENTION

MONTHLY CONTRIBUTIONS TO INVESTMENT ACCOUNT(S)

$200,000	($34,985)	($13,910)	($7,037)	($3,846)	($2,167)
$175,000	($30,612)	($12,171)	($6,157)	($3,365)	($1,896)
$150,000	($26,239)	($10,432)	($5,278)	($2,884)	($1,625)
$125,000	($21,866)	($8,694)	($4,398)	($2,404)	($1,354)
$100,000	($17,493)	($6,955)	($3,519)	($1,923)	($1,083)
$75,000	($13,119)	($5,216)	($2,639)	($1,442)	($813)
$50,000	($8,746)	($3,477)	($1,759)	($961)	($542)
$25,000	($4,373)	($1,739)	($880)	($481)	($271)
	10	20	30	40	50

ANNUAL EXPENSES (TODAY'S DOLLARS)

YEARS TO RETIREMENT (THE DATE WHEN YOU WILL STOP WORKING)

Please, whatever you do, keep in mind that these are estimates. In no way will your retirement savings target be accurate. At the time of this writing, there is no way to guarantee an 8 percent annualized return, and it's impossible to know what inflation will be. The 2.5 percent inflation estimate is based on historical inflation. Investment returns and inflation going forward could rise or fall. This is just a guide. Life happens, so be prepared to change and adapt. By charting a course and working toward these goals today, you will be better equipped to navigate through life's inevitable twists and turns.

When setting goals, don't worry about having every detail worked out. The only certainty in life is uncertainty, and every minute obsessing over the details of your life five years from now is wasting time. What was your five-year plan five years ago? What were your goals? Where did you see yourself living? What was your future job? Did it turn out exactly as planned? Probably not. You may have the intended outcome, but in no way did it work out step-by-step according to the plan.

Successful goal setting strikes the right balance of being clear, achievable, and time-bound, while being flexible enough so that you're not anchored or dependent on a specific reality, outcome, or result. The trick is to make wealth goals a part of who you are by aligning goals with your values, intentions, and actions. If not, your money and wealth will be at risk of being taken from you. Be aware that there are a lot of people trying to get their hands on your hard-earned money.

CHAPTER 11

It's Not What You Make; It's What You Keep

"The money you have gives you freedom; the money you pursue enslaves you."

—JEAN-JACQUES ROUSSEAU

Excited for your next paycheck? Do you know who else is? It's a long list.

- The government. They get first dibs on your paycheck through payroll taxes.
- Next, senior citizens through Social Security taxes.
- Next up on the list? Your health insurance company.
- Next, your landlord or mortgage company.
- Next, your credit cards.

- Next, your public utilities.
- And the list goes on. Most of us never actually get paid.

TIME IN EXCHANGE FOR MONEY

How much money did you spend last month, and how much value did you get out of each expense? Do you even know, or are you just going through the motions, blindly spending with little thought into how much joy, satisfaction, and value you get from each expense? Money is freedom. It affords you the ability to call the shots on how you use your time. When you have money, you can pursue opportunities that provide meaning and purpose such as start a new company, create art, volunteer, or advance your knowledge. Time is yours, and new and exciting opportunities are possible.

But most of us aren't free. We are forced into an expensive trade of time for money. We trade one or two hours each day commuting, eight to ten hours at a job, and another hour or so "detoxing" from the time spent commuting and working.

SPENDING = UNITS OF TIME

When money leaves your wallet, you're trading units

of time for the good being consumed. If you make $60,000 annually, it translates to roughly $25 to $30 per hour. So, that $100 purchase is more than just $100 leaving your wallet—it's four hours of your future time. Time that's nonrenewable and eroding each minute, hour, day, month, and year.

KNOW WHERE YOUR MONEY IS GOING

In my fifteen years of working with high-net-worth individuals, the most common question I get is "What do self-made millionaires have in common?" My answer is that they know where their money is going. Do you know where your money is going? If you don't, you're at risk of making other people rich.

Track expenses however you see fit. Use an app, keep a notebook, or log everything in a spreadsheet. Divide your expenses into three categories: fixed, variable, and periodic. I personally update my expenses every day in a spreadsheet. Having a daily budgeting practice allows me to control my finances from a position of strength.

FIXED EXPENSES

These are payments that rarely change month-to-month such as rent/mortgage, student loans, phone

401(K) PLAN

A 401(k) plan is a retirement account that you own, but your company administers it. You control the account, and if you ever leave, the money comes with you. Most companies offer a 401(k) match.

Let's say your annual salary is $60,000, and your company offers a dollar-for-dollar 401(k) match up to 5 percent. If you contribute 5 percent, $125 is taken directly out of your paycheck (assuming a semimonthly pay schedule) and deposited into your account ($3,000 total for the year), and your company matches it with an additional $3,000. If you contribute $1,000, your company matches $1,000. If you contribute $0, your company matches $0. If you miss out on receiving the maximum match, you're literally saying no to free money. And since contributions are deducted before you receive your paycheck, the money never hits your checking account. So, you can't spend it! A 401(k) is a great savings tool because it makes saving and investing easy to manage and automate. Keep in mind that you are in control over how much you save and invest. Nobody can or will do it for you.

If you're young and have a time horizon that's greater than twenty years, your 401(k) should be heavily invested in stock mutual funds. If you want to make the administration of your 401(k) as easy as possible, most 401(k) plans offer "target date funds." These are funds that change their risk profile over time to be more aggressive when you're young and more conservative as you age. Just pick the date that is closest to your anticipated retirement age (around sixty-five to seventy years old).

Whatever you do with your 401(k), just follow these two rules: 1) set your contribution percentage to be equal to or more than your employer's match and 2) make sure your 401(k) is not held in cash or invested too conservatively. Doing so will cost you over the long term and delay your future retirement date.

bills, gym memberships, car payments, 401(k) contributions, and any monthly contributions to various saving/investment accounts. Yes, monthly savings (including 401(k) contributions) should be a component of your fixed expenses because you need to make sure you're getting paid before everyone else!

VARIABLE EXPENSES

These are standard expenses that occur monthly, such as food, utilities, or entertainment, but the amounts fluctuate.

PERIODIC EXPENSES

These are rare, nonrecurring expenses such as vacations, medical bills, vet bills, or car repairs.

Here is an example of my firm's monthly money tracker:

FUTURE YOU WEALTH
SAVE, INVEST, AND SPEND WITH INTENTION

YOUR NAME
MONTHLY VALUE STATEMENT
DATE

INCOME

	After Tax Paychecks	$4,000.00	
	401(k) Contribution	$625.00	
INCOME TOTAL			$4,625.00

FIXED EXPENSES

	Rent/Mortgage	$1,200.00	
	Student Loans	$300.00	
	Gym	$100.00	
	Phone	$120.00	
	Car Payment (including insurance)	$350.00	
	401(k)	$625.00	
	Investment Account	$300.00	
	Vacation Fund	$200.00	
TOTAL FIXED EXPENSES			$3,195.00

VARIABLE EXPENSES

	Food	$500.00	
	Entertainment	$300.00	
	Household Expenses	$170.00	
	Personal Maintenance	$35.00	
	Clothes	$50.00	
	Amazon/Bulk Delivery	$100.00	
	Pet Supplies	$40.00	
	Transportation (cabs, ride share, train, bus)	$35.00	
	Cash (ATM withdrawal)	$200.00	
TOTAL VARIABLE			$1,430.00

PERIODIC EXPENSES

	Travel	$0.00	
	Health	$0.00	
	Misc	$0.00	
TOTAL PERIODIC			$0.00
TOTAL EXPENSES			$4,625.00
TOTAL INCOME MINUS TOTAL EXPENSES			$0.00

PAY YOURSELF FIRST

Ever get to the end of the year and ask, "Where did all my money go?" Happens all the time and across all income brackets.

Why is this?

Because life happens, and when life gets busy, priorities shift.

Thus, we need simple rules in place when it comes to savings, and the best and easiest rule to follow is to pay yourself first.

It's worth repeating. Commit to moving a minimum set amount each month to your savings goals. Establish a separate savings or investment account for each goal, and automate contributions. Most banks allow you to set up recurring payments. Think of these savings buckets as another expense, and write the contributions into your monthly budget as a fixed expense. Paying yourself first works because it reduces your disposable income, which means you're getting paid before you have an opportunity to spend your hard-earned money.

Commit to tracking expenses by hand (or in a spreadsheet) for the next three months. Set aside time each week to evaluate progress and identify trends and habits that are taking you away from your goals. Yes, it will require time, energy, and commitment, but no one ever said building wealth was easy.

When going through this exercise, look for wasteful themes and identify expenses that can be eliminated. Is there a monthly subscription service that provides little value? Are rideshare costs adding up? Are food expenses piling up? For each expense, ask yourself, "What am I trying to accomplish with this expense?" Areas that are particularly vulnerable are going out to eat, daily habitual purchases, and buying new clothes.

GOING OUT TO EAT

Think about the last time you went out to dinner with friends. How much did it cost? Including drinks, probably between $50 to $100. Perhaps more. Going out to eat can add up, and fast.

What did you value most out of the meal? The drinks? The food? The tablecloths?

No!

The value is in the time spent with friends. Going out to eat is a way to get out of your home and spend time with people that matter. If the real objective is to be together, why not pick a restaurant that provides the right ambiance for the lowest price? Or alternate hosting dinner? You'll be with the same people, have the same conversation, but spend a lot less money.

LATTES

Lattes have become a metaphor for the small habitual purchase that adds up over time. It can be anything. So, if a latte isn't your thing, just think of any daily purchase in the $4 to $10 range. If you look at the cost of the daily $4 to $10 habit, it adds up fast. We're talking anywhere from $1,460 to $3,650 over the course of a year.

Sure, you may get some value out of the daily routine, but there's a good chance that you're on autopilot and just going through the motions. Expensive motions. Diverting expenses away from the daily habitual purchase and rerouting that money toward a savings goal could be the difference between an average vacation and your dream vacation. It could also be the difference between having a daily latte and an extra $1 million in forty years (more on this later). Feels like a long way from now (and it is), but you're sacrificing so little in the short term. A treat here and there won't hurt you financially, and it's fun to indulge from time to time, but be aware that this daily habit could cost you millions over the long term.

CLOTHES

The sweater in your closet that's so last season was once a fun new possession. How long did it last? Probably a couple of months.

Are you attached to a brand or willing to pay a premium for a certain designer?

Why?

It's all the same stuff. Most major brands source their materials and labor from a handful of factories.

It's easy to unknowingly spend $3,000 to $5,000 annually on clothes, all to repeat it again the next year. So, when it comes to clothes, what do we value? No need to break the bank to look good, feel good, and express your own personal style. This doesn't need to be expensive because style is all about quality and fit. The brand name holds little value. The brand premium is to subsidize their image, advertising, and store locations. That's it. Don't fall for it. Your personal value is not tied up in a brand identity.

TURN YOUR BUDGET INTO A VALUE STATEMENT

Tracking expenses, finding less expensive alternatives, and creating financial goals looks and smells like a budget.

But you're not operating under a budget; you're living in accordance with your values. So, your budget is really more of a value statement. A value statement says yes to goals, people, and experiences that bring sustainable value and no to mindless and wasteful "things" that take up space. And here's something you don't hear every day: saving money is fun!

CHAPTER 12

Gamification of Spending

"In every job that must be done, there is an element of fun."

—MARY POPPINS

We love games and competition.

Competition brings out our best and forces us to improve.

Competition is rewarding and challenging.

Competition drives us forward and sets us back.

Competition breeds confidence and humility.

We need competition. Without it, we're just existing.

When you compete, you need an opponent. Someone (or something) that pushes you, scares you, and makes you want (and need) to get better.

PELOTON

Founded in 2012, Peloton, the exercise equipment and media company, has close to $1 billion in revenue and is already a publicly traded company.

On the surface, Peloton is an exercise bike. But any Peloton user will tell you it's so much more. Why? The sleek design? No. The convenience? No. The prestige? No. It's the community, and, most importantly, the leaderboard and data. Peloton tracks your results and compares you to users from around the country in real time. You're able to compete from the comfort of your own home and attempt to beat the *you* of yesterday. Peloton has made a game out of exercise, and it's working. According to Peloton, 96 percent of its users remain subscribers, and its bikes are used an average of thirteen times per month.

EXPENSES

So, if gamification can work for exercise, it can certainly work for managing our expenses. We just need to make it fun.

NO SPENDING DAY

Try to go an entire day without spending—not even a penny.

Yes, it will require some planning and advanced spending such as buying groceries in advance, bringing lunch to work, and making sure household items are well stocked, but it will prevent you from making random impulse purchases—auto-pilot expenditures you don't need. Why is a "No Spending Day" fun? Because it forces you to use your resources and embrace your creativity.

CASH WEEK

Track how much you spend in a typical month on food, clothes, household expenses, and personal maintenance, and divide by four. Take that number and reduce it by 25 percent. Now, on Monday morning, take that number and get cash out of the ATM. This is your spending for the week. For example, if these expenses average $1,200 per month, do the following:

$1,200/4 = $300

$300 x (1-.25) = $225

$225 is your spending for the week. All cash.

Why does this work?

Because using cash forces you to feel the pain of spending your hard-earned money. Next week, reduce the number by another 25 percent. See how far you can go.

HAPPY HOUR MONTH

We need human connection. Having trusted friends and being a part of a community is a key component to living a full and meaningful life, and it's not uncommon to meet over food and drinks. But, as we established, going out to eat can get expensive. So, how about creating a challenge to find places and times with happy hour pricing? Two-for-one drinks and half off the bar menu can cut your restaurant budget in half, but you still get to experience the joy of spending time with friends. After all, that's the real objective.

JUST SAY NO MONTH

Try a month where you deprive yourself of something new. Say no to new clothes, new memberships, new subscriptions, travel, etc. Make do with what you have. The reality is, we all have so much more than we need.

"Just Say No Month" may sound extreme, but it's not.

What's extreme is maxing out your credit card to accumulate more stuff.

SIMPLE DINNER TUESDAY, WEDNESDAY, AND THURSDAY

Tired after a long day? Not up for cooking? Feel the urge for takeout...again?

I've been there. Takeout can get expensive. If we're talking delivery, add on even more. All for subpar food that's forgotten about by the time you sit on the couch. So, if we're talking about food that provides zero lasting value, why not make it cheap and easy? Rice, beans, and an avocado, a simple sandwich, or chicken and broccoli. Try it out in the middle of the week when nothing exciting is happening.

CREATE COMMUNITY

Talk to your friends about the spending challenge(s) you embrace, and make these challenges a community effort. Have fun, compete against each other, and segregate your savings (winnings). By making a game out of saving money, you will start to notice that saving is less about being restrictive and more about taking back control.

DO YOU WANT A RAISE?

Who doesn't? Raises make us feel valued, increase our self-esteem, prove our worth, and are a proxy for how our time is valued.

Think of the last time you got a raise. Were you surprised? Did it change your life? For some, the answer is yes. For some, a raise can be a life-altering event that paves the way for long lasting and sustainable, positive change. For others, the excitement wears off after a few paychecks. After we settle into our "post-raise" life, we're anxious for the next raise cycle. Then, the process repeats.

After your last raise, did you save any more money? Probably not. Why? Because of a phenomenon known as lifestyle creep.

LIFESTYLE CREEP

Think of where you were five to ten years ago. How much money did you make? How much did you spend? What did you spend your money on? Now, think of where you are today. Do you make more? Do you spend more? Do you have more financial obligations?

Lifestyle creep occurs when a larger paycheck becomes

an invitation to develop more expensive habits, hobbies, and tastes such as buying a bigger home, a luxury car, or an exclusive gym membership.

The spiral feeds itself and before you know it, the new expenses outpace the increase of the raise. Forget about being excited for the next raise; you are now desperate for a salary hike.

GIVE YOURSELF A RAISE

Waiting for your boss to give you a raise? How about giving yourself a raise today by carving out more to your bottom line (the money you keep)?

Let's take an example of a single California resident who makes $60,000 per year. We assume she pays $100 each paycheck for health insurance and contributes 3 percent to her 401(k).

Given these assumptions, her semimonthly paycheck is approximately $1,700, or $3,400 each month. If she were to get a raise of $10,000, her semimonthly paycheck would increase to approximately $1,930, or $3,860 each month. So, a $10,000 annual raise would net her an additional $460 each month.

What if she could carve out an additional $460 this month without getting a raise?

Would this be impossible to accomplish? Probably not. That's $15 a day. An extra $460 could come down to eliminating a few monthly subscription services, bringing lunch to work, finding a less expensive gym membership, moving to a less expensive apartment, walking or taking public transportation instead of ride-sharing, etc. No matter what cuts she makes, reducing monthly expenses by $460 will have the same impact as receiving a $10,000 raise.

How about a $15,000 raise? Reduce monthly expenses by $700 ($22 per day). Want a $20,000 raise? Reduce monthly expenses by $930 ($30 per day).

Yes, by getting an actual raise she would be able to contribute more to her 401(k), but you get the point. It's about taking control.

While carving out more to your "bottom line" is a great strategy, there is a limit to the amount you can cut.

So, what can you do if you want an even bigger raise?

INCREASE YOUR EARNINGS!

I'm not talking about earnings from your current job. I'm talking about a side hustle. Is there anything you could be doing on the side to earn some extra cash?

Enjoy basketball? Can you make an extra $50 to $100 per week being a referee? All it takes is one night a week and/or a couple of hours over the weekend.

Do you love playing the guitar? Can you give part-time lessons?

Love dogs? Do you have thirty to sixty minutes a day to take on a couple of dog walking clients?

There's Uber, Lyft, DoorDash, Wag, Rover, and even selling goods on Etsy. In today's world, it's easier than ever to earn supplemental income.

The point is, stop waiting for your boss, and give *yourself* a raise. The only person you need permission from is *you*.

MAKE IT FUN

Whatever you do, make saving and budgeting fun. I hear excuses all the time—"It's impossible to save."

No, it's just that you're not trying to save.

USING YOUR MONEY TO MAKE MORE MONEY

Financially independent versus financially insecure. What's the difference?

Financially independent people have control over their time. They're free from the chains of a monthly paycheck and can live each day in alignment with their values.

How?

Because their money is working for them.

The financially independent say no to instant gratification and pleasure. They embrace an abundance mindset, identify what they want, free themselves from unhealthy attachments, and define wealth on their terms. The financially independent also say no to mindless consumption and yes to ownership.

Most of us do the opposite. We overspend on depreciating assets like clothes, furniture, and cars. This "stuff" loses value each day, week, month, and year. It's this overaccumulation of depreciating assets that keeps us living as suppliers of labor—exchanging our time for money and waiting for our bosses to give us a raise—all because we take our hard-earned money to buy "stuff" that loses value. It's a terrible trade, but you can change the script by owning appreciating (increasing in value) and/or income-producing assets.

Stocks, real estate, and bonds (lending money) all pay dividends while their owners sleep. Ownership is the secret to building wealth. More specifically, owning the "stuff" that appreciates and/or pays an income stream over time.

CHAPTER 13

The Stock Market

"Everyone has the brainpower to follow the stock market. If you made it through fifth-grade math, you can do it."

—PETER LYNCH

The stock market is (and has been) the single biggest contributor to wealth over time. Stock returns have outpaced those of cash, bonds, real estate, commodities, and collectibles. It's not even close.

What is a stock, and what does it mean to own a stock?

Quite simply, when you buy a stock, you own a piece of a company. If you buy shares of Apple, you are now a partial owner (shareholder). You can walk into an Apple store and watch people buying products from *your* company.

THE STOCK MARKET · 161

And as Apple grows as a company, your wealth grows along with it. Exciting, right? It gets even better because most large, well-established companies take part of their profits and give it back to shareholders in the form of a dividend. In other words, you get paid to own stocks.

The combination of capital appreciation and dividends is called an investor's "total return." Over a typical twenty-year period, total annual stock market returns have averaged anywhere between 8 and 10 percent. This translates into your money doubling every seven to ten years. Why? It's due to the power of compounding. Don't believe it? The math doesn't lie.

THE POWER OF COMPOUNDING

Let's say you invest $100 and experience a 10 percent annualized return for the next seven years. At the end of year one, you'll have $110 ($100 x .10 = $10, $100 + $10 = $110).

In year two, the stock market once again appreciates by 10 percent, but this time, you started with a base of $110. So, instead of earning $10, you earn $11 and end the year with $121 ($110 x .10 = $11, $110 + $11 = $121).

Year 3: 10 percent return on $121—end the year with $133.10.

Year 4: 10 percent return on $131.10—end the year with $146.41.

Year 5: 10 percent return on $146.41—end the year with $161.05.

Year 6: 10 percent return on $161.05—end the year with $177.16.

Year 7: 10 percent return on 177.16—end the year with $194.87.

In seven years, your initial investment of $100 almost doubled.

As a side note, the stock market does not provide a guaranteed or steady return of 8 to10 percent. That's just the average return over time. The stock market could be up 20 percent in year one, and down -10 percent in year two. More on this coming up.

Let's revisit the lattes. You know, the daily habitual $4 to $10 purchase. Assuming a stock market return of 10 percent (based on historical returns), saying no to the daily latte and yes to investing $5 a day ($150 per month) in the stock market would result in over $950,000 in forty years. All it takes is $5 a day to experience this powerful wealth-building force. The stock market is not reserved for the rich. They are just the ones benefiting.

So, why aren't people taking advantage?

It's because we're confused, intimidated, and time constrained. The investment industry and financial media want you to believe that investing in stocks is complex, and that you need to pay high fees for "sophisticated" advice. This is far from the truth.

When it comes to the stock market, the simplest approach almost always leads to the best outcomes. You just need to follow four simple rules:

1. Diversify using low-cost index funds.
2. Invest in consistent increments.
3. Stay invested over the long run.
4. Minimize fees and emotions.

DIVERSIFY USING LOW-COST INDEX FUNDS

Diversification can be summed up by the old saying:

"Don't put all your eggs in one basket." Owning just one stock exposes you to the ups and downs of a single company—a company that may be hot today, but obsolete tomorrow. Hindsight is 20/20, and it's easy to look back and rationalize how clear and obvious it was that Apple, Amazon, and Microsoft would go on to become such massive successes. Yet, it's nearly impossible to decipher the next Amazon from the next Pets.com. Even the pros get it wrong. So, instead of owning just one stock, own many.

Don't have time to research, trade, and manage such a big responsibility? Most of us don't, but there's a quick, easy, and effective approach that beats 90 percent of the pros.

Just buy and hold low-cost index funds.

WHAT IS AN INDEX FUND?

Let's go all the way back to 1923. A publisher of financial reports and analysis, Standard & Poor's, created a proxy for the US stock market. It started with just a small number of stocks but quickly expanded. Today, this proxy includes the largest five hundred stocks and is known as the S&P 500. It's the industry proxy for the US stock market, and you can own all five hundred

stocks in just a single purchase. How? By owning an
S&P 500 Index Fund.

Popularized by the legendary mutual fund company
Vanguard, index funds pool money from investors and
buy shares in all five hundred stocks represented in the
index. So, if you buy shares in an S&P 500 index fund,
you are a partial owner of Apple, Facebook, Google,
Microsoft, Proctor & Gamble, and the list goes on.
Since the fund company takes a "passive" approach
(all they must do is replicate the index), fees are typically low. Most S&P 500 index funds charge fees of
one-tenth of a percent (.10 percent) or less: for every
$100 invested, the fund charges $0.10.

Buying an S&P 500 index fund or exchange traded fund
(ETFs are a close cousin to the index fund; index funds
trade once per day, while ETFs trade intraday (multiple
trades within a day) is an easy and cost-effective way to
get diversified exposure to the US stock market. When
you own an S&P 500 index fund, you are tied to the
growth of the economy.

It doesn't end with the S&P 500. There are thousands
of stock market index funds (and ETFs) ranging from
funds that provide exposure to non-US developed economies such as Europe, Australia, and the Far East, to

emerging market economies. There are sector-specific index funds (index funds that just focus on technology stocks) and trend-focused funds (funds that invest in companies that are popular with Millennials). To keep it simple, just focus on index funds that are linked to the S&P 500 for US stocks, MSCI EAFE (Europe, Australia, and the Far East) for non-US stocks, and funds that are managed by well-known investment companies (Vanguard, Fidelity, and iShares by Blackrock).

PASSIVE INDEX FUNDS VERSUS ACTIVE FUNDS

Can it really be this easy? Just buy and hold low-cost index funds? There must be a way to get an "edge," right?

Well, when you look at the numbers, the "less is more" path to investing yields the best results.

Each year, Standard & Poor's releases a report on how active managers do against their passive benchmarks. The results aren't good.

In 2018, 64.5 percent of active (professional) large cap managers lagged the S&P 500.

Extend the time period out ten years, and it gets worse

with a projected 85.1 percent of active large cap managers lagging the S&P 500.

Extend out fifteen years, and 91.6 percent of active large cap managers will likely lag the S&P 500.[11]

The average person can save time, energy, and money by just investing in passive, low-cost index funds. You can go on with your life and beat more than 90 percent of the investing pros in the process.

INVEST IN CONSISTENT INCREMENTS

Is it better to invest now or wait for a better entry point? Yes, and yes.

How?

By investing today, and again in a month, and again the month after. It's a process called Dollar Cost Averaging. Dollar Cost Averaging spreads out timing risk, builds good saving habits, and takes the thought and emotion out of the investing process. Does this sound familiar? Well, if you participate in a 401(k) plan, it's the exact same concept.

---

11   S&P Dow Jones Indices. https://us.spindices.com/spiva/#/reports.

Building wealth through the stock market is a process. It's a series of steps. The stock market is not a get-rich-quick scheme. There are ups and downs, and the rewards go to those who ignore the noise and stick to the process. Actually, it's a lot like travel.

Have you ever traveled to a far destination? Perhaps you took a flight to another continent or went on a cross-country road trip. Remember the experience?

Traveling is almost always rewarding and enlightening, but getting there can be a hassle. Traveling takes time, patience, planning, and commitment, but you can embrace the process in a positive way.

Think about the process of traveling overseas. After months of planning, the day finally arrives. You pack a suitcase and head to the airport only to find long security lines and potential delays. Next, you board a plane and sit in a confined space for hours. After you land, you claim your stuff, catch a cab/bus/train to your destination, and check in to your lodging accommodations. Hours later, you're experiencing the true joy of travel; the process and pain it took to arrive is long forgotten.

Building wealth is no different. It's just a series of steps. At first, it will appear as if you're running in place. Just keep moving and trust the process. Your plane will eventually land, and you will arrive at your destination. Let's run through a scenario.

CASE STUDY: JODY, THE YOUNG INVESTOR

Jody started her wealth-building journey in July 2006. She knew nothing about the stock market, so she kept it simple by investing in a low-cost S&P 500 index fund and made a commitment to investing $500 at the end of each month. She ignored all stock market news and stuck with the process.

How much did she have on June 30, 2019? Let's look back at her journey. After year one, her balance was $6,469. Good, but not life changing.

Year two? Her balance was $11,072, but after total contributions of $12,000.

Year three? It was $14,112, but after total contributions of $18,000. It's kind of like being excited to travel out of the country only to be hit with a three-hour delay. Frustrated and going nowhere.

Fast forward to year six with a balance of $43,303. Making progress.

Year ten? $101,332.

After thirteen years, and contributions of $78,000, her account value is over $171,000. Not enough to retire on, but a strong foundation. All from just a simple process—investing in low-cost index funds, and a $500 contribution at the end of each month. So, why aren't more people doing this? Let's look at some common excuses.

> "This is great for the person who was smart enough to start at age twenty-two. I'm thirty-five and have no savings. I'm already far behind! Feels like I'll never catch up!"

If this is you, you're not alone, but if you're kicking yourself for not starting thirteen years ago, how do you think you'll feel in thirteen years if you don't start *today*? Think you'll look back at thirty-five-year-old you and say, "Good thing you didn't start at thirty-five since you were already behind." No! You'll say, "I really should have started when I had the chance at thirty-five!" If you start today, Future You will be thanking Present Day You. It doesn't matter if you're late to the journey. You may never fully catch up to the person who started at age twenty-two, but it doesn't matter. Just start the process and create your own benchmarks. You won't be rich overnight, and you will certainly experience delays and bumps along the way, but the destination will be more than worth it.

> "I have the worst timing and I just know if I put my money in the stock market today, it's going to drop. I think I should wait."

While market corrections and bear markets are painful, they're part of the process. Accept it and keep moving. Don't cancel your trip over a three-hour delay. Jody started in 2006, right before the financial crisis. She didn't wait for the financial crisis to pass. She didn't stop the process when things got tough. She ignored the noise, and her patience and commitment were rewarded. There were times when she contributed $500 right before a stock market rally, and times when she contributed $500 right before a sell-off. In the end, it all evened out.

What if she experienced nothing but bad timing? What if she had the worst luck? Let's run through an alternative scenario, but this time, instead of investing $500 at the end of each month, she'll contribute a lump sum of $6,000 once a year at the worst possible time.

- $6,000 in September 2007—The peak before the bear market caused by the Great Recession. The stock market would drop another 40-plus percent.

- $6,000 in August 2008—Two weeks before the collapse of Lehman Brothers.
- $6,000 in March 2010—At the start of the Eurozone debt crisis.
- $6,000 in April 2011—Three months before the debt ceiling debate that pushed the stock market into correction territory.

And so on. The top of the stock market for each twelve-month period. The worst security line, the only flight that experienced delays, bad cab drivers, etc.

How much does she have after thirteen years of terrible timing?

$153,000!

There were certainly more bumps and setbacks along the way, but this is still a solid base to build on.

Every journey is a series of steps. Ignore the distance, embrace the process, and have faith that even the most distant destinations get closer with every step. By investing in consistent increments, you spread out your timing risk, continually build on your existing base, and develop healthy saving and investing habits that add up over time. This brings us to our next rule: stay invested.

STAY INVESTED OVER THE LONG TERM

There are two times when the value of the stock market matters: when you buy and when you sell. Other than that, the day-to-day fluctuations are just noise.

Picture something of value you own (a house, valuable art, or ownership in a small business) and imagine someone yelling out different prices into a megaphone for six and a half hours a day. Would you panic and sell when the person yelled out a lower price? Would you rush to buy when the when the person yelled out a higher price? No! To the extent possible, you would ignore this lunatic and tell them to get off your lawn.

Well, this is the stock market. Between the hours of 9:30 a.m. to 4:00 p.m. EDT, traders yell out the prices of public companies. It's a lot of noise, and for a long-term investor these prices hold zero significance. Down days are just paper losses. If you don't sell into the noise, you don't lose anything.

The best thing you can do during times of market panic is turn off the TV, ignore the news, and do something fun and productive. Play with your kids or pets, go for a walk or run, go fishing, or whatever else you can do to avoid getting wrapped up in the noise and panic.

Yes, the stock market comes with risk, but over time the odds are in your favor. Just look at these statistics:

1. THE STOCK MARKET IS UP MORE THAN IT'S DOWN.

From 1950 to 2018, the stock market has been up fifty-four out of sixty-nine years (78 percent of calendar years)[12] and gains have been significant. A $1,000 investment made at the start of 1950 would be worth close to $1,500,000 at the end of 2018. All for doing nothing. You get rewarded for patience.

On a given day, the stock market is up about 53 percent of the time. Extend the time period out to three months, and the stock market is up around 66 percent of the time, and over a rolling twelve-month period, 75 percent of the time. So, if you're a long-term investor, make no mistake about it, you will experience some down days, weeks, months, and years. If you stay invested for the long term, you'll experience more up days than down days. You just need to be patient.

---

12 Aswath Damodaran, "Annual Returns on Stock, T. Bonds, and T. Bills: 1928–Current, New York University Stern School of Business, January 5, 2019, http://pages.stern.nyu. edu/~adamodar/New_Home_Page/datafile/histretSP.html.

2. BE PREPARED FOR SHORT-TERM LOSSES. ON AVERAGE, THE STOCK MARKET EXPERIENCES A PEAK-TO-TROUGH LOSS OF GREATER THAN 10 PERCENT EVERY ONE TO TWO YEARS.

Over the last sixty-nine years, the stock market has dropped more than 10 percent on thirty-seven different occasions.[13] Translation: expect a peak-to-trough decline of more than 10 percent to happen within the next two years. Your wealth journey will experience delays and setbacks. Don't sell into the panic. Instead, thank the market for the 10 percent drop. Why? Because it's the reason you get paid over time. Volatility weeds out the weak from the strong, and the strong get rewarded.

3. LOSSES ARE MADE UP QUICKLY.

Since 1950, the average time to recovery for a loss of greater than 10 percent is six months.[14]

MINIMIZE FEES AND EMOTIONS

It's not what you earn, but what you keep that matters.

---

13 Edward Yardeni, Joe Abbott, and Mali Quintana, *Market Briefing: S&P 500 Bull & Bear Markets & Corrections*, Yardeni Research, Inc., December 18, 2019, https://www.yardeni.com/pub/sp500corrbear.pdf.

14 Yardeni, Abbot, and Quintana, https://www.yardeni.com/pub/sp500corrbear.pdf.

The areas that erode the most wealth over time are fees and emotions.

When it comes to having a relationship with a financial advisor, it's common to pay two layers of fees. The first layer is for advice. This fee is for the planning, coaching, and expertise surrounding their investment strategy and asset allocation. Fees are paid by the hour, a flat monthly fee, or as a percentage of assets. The most common fee is a percentage of assets. For this fee structure, the first fee layer ranges from .25 percent to 2 percent. The second fee layer goes to the mutual fund company (or outside manager) the advisor selects on your behalf. These fees range from as low as .03 percent for passive funds to as high as 2 percent for actively managed funds.

Put the two layers together, and fees are all across the board—from .28 percent on the low side to 4 percent on the high side. Most fees are somewhere between 1 to 2 percent of assets under management. To be clear, there's nothing nefarious about charging two layers of fees. It's the industry standard, and it's in the client's best interest for their advisor to allocate funds to outside investment managers. Doing so provides your advisor more time to work with you on planning and coaching. That said, it's important for clients to be aware of the layers and to ask for the total "all-in fee" (the fee that includes all fee layers) at the start of the relationship. The more you pay, the less you keep.

Let's look at an example using an all-in fee of 2 percent. If a client starts with $50,000, contributes $1,000 each month, and earns an after-fee return of 5 percent per year (compounded monthly), they would have $1,890,000 at the end of forty years.

How would this look if they worked with an advisor that employed the same investment strategy, but with an all-in fee of 1 percent? The client would have $2,540,000 at the end of forty years. That's $650,000 more!

Does this mean you need to avoid financial advisors? If you are organized with your money, know your goals and are good about holding yourself accountable to meet those goals, comfortable implementing and managing an investment strategy, aware of the different savings and investment vehicles; familiar with insurance options, and have the discipline to stick with the investment strategy during challenging market environments, then yes, you are wasting money with a financial advisor.

But investing is emotional and when it comes to making

money, emotions are our worst enemy. Each year, the financial consulting firm DALBAR releases the investing results for the "average investor," and the results aren't good. Instead of following the old adage of "buy low and sell high," the average investor does the opposite. The average investor tends to get excited during good times and buys more stocks (buy high) and panics during stock market corrections and sells (sell low). Over time, emotions have been the biggest destroyer of wealth, and we can see it in the data.

According to the 2017 DALBAR Study,[15] in 2016, the stock market returned 11.96 percent, but the average stock market investor returned 7.26 percent. Extend the time period out ten years, and we see a similar story. At the end of 2016, the ten-year annualized return of the stock market was 6.95 percent, but the average investor returned a dismal 3.64 percent. Extend the time period out twenty years, and the average investor loses out again. The twenty-year annualized return of the stock market was 7.68 percent, but the average investor returned just 4.79 percent. Finally, extend the time period out thirty years, and we see a recurring theme. The thirty-year annualized return of the stock market

15   "Quantitative Analysis of Investor Behavior," DALBAR, https://www.dalbar.com/QAIB/ Index; Lance Roberts, "Dalbar 2017: Investors Suck at Investing & Tips for Advisors, RIA: Real Investment Advice, September 25, 2017, https://realinvestmentadvice.com/ dalbar-2017-investors-suck-at-investing-tips-for-advisors/.

was 10.1 percent, but the average investor returned 3.98 percent.

Translated into actual dollars, the gap is truly alarming. If you invested $100,000 in the S&P 500 on 12/31/1986 and did nothing for thirty years, you would have $1,820,000 at the end of 2016. But if you were the average investor, you would end the thirty-year period with just $322,000. That's $1.5 million less! If you are comfortable investing on your own, just be mindful of the biggest threat of all—your emotions.

The stock market gets a bad reputation for being risky, confusing, and exclusive, but this is far from the truth.

To recap, the stock market is an inclusive and powerful force for building wealth, and you can beat 90 percent of the pros by following just four simple rules:

1. Diversify using low-cost index funds.
2. Invest in consistent increments.
3. Stay invested over the long run.
4. Minimize fees and emotions.

It's that easy.

CHAPTER 14

Real Estate

"If I were to write an autobiography called: "My Life—10 Miserable Moments," owning a home would be two of them."

—JAMES ALTUCHER

Home ownership. The path to riches, right? Well, not exactly.

Home ownership can be a positive goal for individuals and society at large. Home ownership breeds a sense of pride and community, has tangible value, and can add to personal wealth. But relying on a home as the primary wealth-building asset can be a risky move. Especially if it's at the expense of owning higher appreciating assets, such as stocks.

Just look at the returns of stocks (represented by the S&P 500) versus residential real estate since 1991. A hundred thousand dollars invested in residential real estate in early 1991 would be worth close to $300,000 today. But that same $100,000 invested in the stock market would be worth over $800,000 today. That's a huge difference![16]

"But with real estate you get the benefit of leverage, right?"

Very true, as most of us borrow to buy real estate. Over time, leverage amplifies the return, but it's still not a compelling reason to own real estate over stocks.

CASE STUDY: REAL ESTATE VERSUS THE STOCK MARKET
INVESTOR A

Investor A buys a $500,000 house by putting $100,000 down and borrowing (taking out a mortgage for) the remaining $400,000. Let's assume the monthly mortgage payment is $2,000 per month for the next thirty years. After twenty-eight years, the house is worth $1,500,000 and Investor A is close to owning it free

---

16   "House Price Index Datasets," Federal Housing Finance Agency, https://www.fhfa.gov/
       DataTools/Downloads/Pages/House-Price-Index-Datasets.aspx#mpo; Andy Kiersz, "Is
       Buying a House a Better Investment than the Stock Market? We Did the Math, and the
       Answer Is Clear," Business Insider, September 15, 2018, https://www.businessinsider.com/
       real-estate-vs-stock-market-investment-2018-9.

and clear. This is a great return! How could the stock market beat that?

INVESTOR B

Investor B also starts with $100,000, but uses $50,000 for a down payment on a $250,000 home and takes the remaining $50,000 and buys an S&P 500 index fund. In this scenario, instead of paying $2,000 per month for a mortgage payment, they pay $1,000, and take the extra $1,000 saved each month to invest in the stock market. Where is Investor B after twenty-eight years? The house is worth $750,000, and their stock portfolio is worth $1,500,000. They have a total net worth of $2,250,000!

Investor B ends up with $750,000 more than Investor A, and this doesn't include the added costs that Investor A would incur from owning a more expensive home (taxes, maintenance, etc.). Owning a home is expensive. More on this later.

The takeaway: stretching past your financial boundaries to buy real estate at the expense of owning stocks could mean leaving money on the table. Whatever you do, do NOT be the person who raids their retirement accounts for a bigger down payment. Instead, buy a more affordable house and remain invested. Can't find the house you need at the current price point? Take more time to save. Renting for a little while longer won't kill you.

PROS AND CONS

What are the pros and cons of home ownership?

PROS:

You Build Equity: When you buy a house, you take ownership of an asset. Taking out a mortgage? Well, part of the payment goes toward paying down the balance of the debt. Translation: each month you get closer to owning the home free and clear. This could be viewed as a form of "forced savings."

Personal Stability: When you buy a house, you're (or at least should be) committing to a place for the long term. This can provide peace and stability. Also, you can make the home yours. There is tremendous pride and personal value in owning a "forever" home.

Price Appreciation: While real estate hasn't seen the same price appreciation as the stock market, it is, over time, an appreciating asset. When you own your home, you get the benefit of shelter along with some price appreciation.

Cost of Carry: Home ownership is expensive. When the fridge breaks down, who is paying for it? You. Taxes? Yes, property taxes are real. Damaged roof? Ouch, that's going to cost you. House need a new paint job? You get the point. And guess what, you don't get any of this money back. When people say you're throwing away money with rent, you throw away a lot of money owning a home too. Before buying a home, make sure to have at least six months of living expenses saved and held in cash. Surprises seem to have the worst timing!

Inferior Investment to Stocks: As we highlighted in the example above, buying real estate at the expense of investing in the stock market can compromise your future wealth.

Leverage Can Work against You: While leverage can work to your benefit, it can also wipe you out. For example, let's say you buy a house for $500,000 with a $100,000 down payment. One year later, the house appreciates by 20 percent and is now worth $600,000. If you sell the house for $600,000 and pay off the

$400,000 mortgage, you are left with $200,000. That's a 100 percent return! Amazing, right?

Well, it works the other way too. If the house depreciates by 20 percent, it is now worth $400,000. If you are forced to sell, $400,000 is used to pay off the mortgage, and you are left with $0. You just lost $100,000!

Bottom Line: Owning a home is beneficial to the extent that:

- You intend to live in the house for at least five years.
- You have a solid emergency savings base.
- You continue to invest in the stock market (at least in retirement accounts).

Owning a home is not a free ride, and it's not the only way to gain exposure to real estate assets.

REAL ESTATE INVESTMENT TRUSTS (REITS)

A REIT is a company that owns and operates income-producing properties. Examples include office buildings, apartments, warehouses, shopping centers, and hotels. REITs are traded just like stocks, and you can buy shares of REITs at any online brokerage firm (Schwab, Fidelity, or e-Trade).

RENTAL PROPERTIES

If you want cash flow you can "touch," try owning rental properties. Instead of buying just one side of a duplex, buy the entire building, live on one side, and rent out the other. If structured in the right way, you may be able to have the rent cover your mortgage. Owning a rental property does, however, come with its fair share of headaches and should be approached with caution.

CROWDFUND PLATFORMS

If owning a rental property is too much of a commitment, there are real estate crowdfunding platforms where you own fractional shares of commercial or residential real estate properties but without the administrative responsibilities for managing a property and tenants.

CHAPTER 15

Bonds (Fixed Income)

"The rich rule over the poor, and the borrower is slave to the lender."

—THE BIBLE, PROVERBS 22:7

Do you have a mortgage? If so, your payments are a combination of principal and interest. Paying down principal gets you closer to owning the home outright, and interest is the cost of money. When you borrow money (take on debt), you are paying someone or something (like a bank) to have access to their money in exchange for a promise that you'll pay them back more over time.

But we're not the only ones who borrow money. Countries, companies, and states/cities/towns also borrow.

And, like you and I, they pay interest on the money they borrow. How do people like you and I become lenders to these countries, companies, and municipalities? By owning bonds.

When you own a bond, you're a lender. Instead of making interest and principal payments, you receive them. Principal payment(s) are how you get your money back, and interest is the amount you earn. The interest rate (the amount you get paid) all depends on the level of risk, and bonds come with two types of risk: credit quality and interest rates.

The more reliable or credit worthy a borrower, the less interest paid (received). The less reliable or credit worthy a borrower, the more interest paid (received). More risk equals more interest. Bonds that have the highest credit quality are US Treasury Bonds. These bonds are backed by the full faith and credit of the US federal government and are considered "risk free."

Bonds are also subject to interest rate risk. If you buy a bond that matures in ten years, you engage in a ten-year contract with the borrower where they agree to pay you a pre-determined interest rate for the duration of the contract. If interest rates increase a day later, lenders now have an opportunity to earn even more interest, but you're out of luck. Why? It's because you're stuck with the lower interest rate established when you bought the bond. The longer the contact, the longer you must wait to invest in a similar bond with the newly established higher interest rate. You could sell the bond and reinvest the proceeds, but the only way someone will buy a bond with a lower interest rate than the market is if they're able to do so at a discount. So, the longer the term (or duration) of the contract, the more interest rate risk.

Thus, like stocks, it's best to diversify your bond holdings by owning bond index funds that have a high credit quality, medium duration, and low fees. It's important to note that, like real estate, bond returns are inferior to stock market returns over the long term. So, if you have a long-term time horizon, bonds should play a small role in your portfolio. Getting paid on your excess cash, it pays to be a lender versus the other way around.

CHAPTER 16

Managing Risk

"You have to take risks. We only understand the miracle of life fully when we allow the unexpected to happen."

—PAULO COELHO

When it comes to financial planning (and life), we need to develop a healthy relationship with risk. What is risk, and how is it defined?

Risk is all about the degree of uncertainty.

When an event or activity is familiar, the less risky we perceive it to be.

When we can understand and quantify the potential for loss, we are less fearful.

Why?

It's because uncertainty is removed. We know what to expect and can anticipate the bends in the road. The activities and events that involve little to no risk are the routine and mundane. There is comfort in the mundane.

On the flip side, when an event or activity is unfamiliar, the riskier we perceive it to be.

When we can't understand or quantify the potential for loss, we are more fearful.

Why?

We have no clue what to expect, and the bends in the road come out of nowhere. Uncertainty makes us feel uncomfortable and out of control. Uncertainty breeds fear.

But with risk comes reward.

Taking calculated risks can be the difference between a comfortable retirement and one filled with financial stress. On the personal side, taking calculated risks can be the difference between living an exciting life versus just existing. Like everything in life, risk requires balance. Too much risk can leave you broken. Too little risk can leave you full of regret. When it comes to investing, how can we strike the right balance?

BALANCING RISK AND RETURN

Investing in appreciating assets involves uncertainty, which, as highlighted earlier, equals risk. But there is an easy way to mitigate the risk: invest according to time horizons.

UNDERSTANDING TIME HORIZONS

There are two types of risk when it comes to investing: losing money and missing out. The risk you're most exposed to all depends on the time horizon for a given goal. As a general rule, short-term goals face the risk of losing money and long-term goals face the risk of missing out.

Short-Term Goals

Let's say you plan to buy a house within the next year and have $100,000 saved for a down payment. Should you invest your $100,000 down payment fund in the stock market? Let's look at the historical range of stock market returns over a one-year period.

Looking back over the last thirty calendar years, the best and worst one-year stock market returns were 37.20 percent and -36.55 percent, respectively. Putting this into real dollars, $100,000 invested in the stock market for just one year could result in $137,200 on the high side or $63,450 on the low side. While there is potential for a larger down payment, there is also a chance your down payment fund will be compromised. Thus, the potential upside is not worth the risk.

Long-Term Goals

Let's say you have $100,000 in excess savings (funds outside of your emergency savings) reserved for retirement in thirty years. Is the stock market appropriate? Let's look back at the historical stock market returns, but this time through a different lens. When you have a thirty-year holding period, the individual year-over-year returns are of less importance. What we really care about is the thirty-year annualized return.

Over the last thirty years, the stock market has annualized at a rate of 10.61 percent. Yes, this includes the low return of -36.55 percent, but it also includes the high return of 37.20 percent. When you smooth the returns out over the entire thirty-year period, bad years are followed by good years, good years are followed bad years, and the odds of experiencing a positive return over the entire thirty-year period is strongly in your favor.

What does this mean in terms of actual dollars? If you invested $100,000 in the stock market thirty years ago, you would have $2.1 million today. Depending on how much you spend, this could provide a nice retirement. If you held the $100,000 in a savings account, you would have around $270,000 today (not enough to retire). Bottom line: when it comes to long-term goals, avoiding the stock market is the risky move.

ASSET ALLOCATION

What's the best mix of assets (stocks, real estate, bonds, etc.) for a given time horizon? Follow this guide:

Short-Term Goals

All short-term savings goals—emergency savings, vacation fund, new furniture—should be held in a high-interest savings account. Don't get cute with this money.

Intermediate-Term Goals

From an asset allocation standpoint, these goals can be tricky.

Goals that are three to five years away should be invested in a more conservative manner. Some stock market exposure is fine, but no more than 30 to 50 percent. The remaining 50 to 70 percent should be invested in high-quality bond funds and/or a high-interest savings account.

Goals that are six to ten years away can be invested more aggressively. Figure 50 to 70 percent to stocks and 30 to 50 percent to a combination of high-quality bond funds, real estate investment trusts (REITs), and high-yield savings.

Long-Term Goals

Goals that are eleven to twenty years away can be invested even more aggressively: 80 to 90 percent to stocks and 10 to 20 percent to a combination of high-quality bond funds and real estate investment trusts (REITs).

Goals that are more than twenty years away should be allocated mostly to stocks because you'll have more than enough time to make up any short-term losses.

Please note that goals are fluid and will change over time. Remember that ten-year goals will eventually turn into two-year goals. Pay attention and adjust accordingly.

PUTTING IT ALL TOGETHER

Like the stock market, when it comes to managing risk and asset allocation the most effective strategy is usually the easiest to implement and manage. Just follow these simple rules (some may sound familiar):

- Diversification—Invest in different types of assets (cash, bonds, real estate, and stocks).
- Match risk with time horizon—Be more conservative for short-term goals (cash and bonds) and more aggressive for long-term goals (stocks).
- Invest in consistent increments over time.
- Remain invested over the long run.
- Minimize fees (and emotions).

Bottom Line: All short-term wealth goals (within the next two years) should be in cash. Wealth goals between three and ten years should be a combination of stocks, real estate investment trusts, bonds, and cash. All long-term wealth goals should be invested primarily in stocks. By taking a goals-based approach to managing risk, you mitigate the competing risks of losing money in the short term and missing out over the long term. The biggest risk of all is to do nothing and just hope it all works out.

CHAPTER 17

Financial Fitness

"No one's ever achieved financial fitness with a January resolution that's abandoned by February."

—SUZE ORMAN

If you feel overwhelmed by money, take comfort in the fact that you're not alone. Starting your wealth-building journey is a scary and uncomfortable process, but there are blogs, books, financial planners, and wealth coaches available to help. If you decide to hire a financial planner or wealth coach, make sure they act under the fiduciary standard (must act in your best interest and are not paid on commissions to push products), and make sure their fees are transparent and easy to understand.

Building wealth is like improving your fitness level, but there's a big difference in knowing when you're financially fit versus being physically fit.

It's easy to know when you're physically fit. You can see it, feel it, and when you notice results, momentum builds and progress fuels more progress. It's a beautiful cycle.

How do you know when you're financially fit? Is it the size of your bank account? What about being debt free? Are you making progress or just spinning your wheels? I've distilled this last chapter down to the six steps to financial fitness.

Step 1—Participate in your company's 401(k) plan up to the employer match. If your company offers a 401(k) plan, contribute up to your employer's match. As a reminder, let's say you make $50,000 annually and your company matches dollar for dollar up to 3 percent. If you contribute up to the match of 3 percent, you will save $3,000 in one year—$1,500 from you, and $1,500 from your company. You get an extra $1,500 for free! To achieve this, you must contribute. No contribution? No free money.

Step 2—Pay off all credit card debt. We all feel when jeans get a little tight around the waistline and know that it's time to cut calories. How do we know when to cut financial calories? When we see credit card debt. Think about it. Like fat, credit card debt is the result of overconsumption. And the more you feed the debt, the bigger the hole, and the harder it is to get back to neutral.

When you consume more calories than you burn, your body stores the excess as fat. When you spend more money than you make, your net worth statement stores the excess as credit card debt. Credit card debt is expensive and will keep you locked in a prison of your own consumption.

If you're drowning in credit card debt, try consolidating your debt through a balance transfer. Most balance transfer offers will give you a rate of around 5 percent for twelve months. By consolidating your debt, you make the process cheaper and easier to manage. Peer-to-peer lending services can also be a nice way to consolidate your debt and lower your interest rate. The trick is to make debt reduction part of your monthly budget. Sure, it will require a change in lifestyle, but the lifestyle is the reason for the debt in the first place. Something's not working and the sooner you make a change, the better.

Step 3—Save up to six months of living expenses for emergencies. As you increase your level of physical activity, an important point of emphasis is your range of motion. In other words, your flexibility.

When it comes to your personal finances, your range of motion is in the form of an emergency savings fund—six months of living expenses held in a high-yield savings account. When you accumulate six months of living expenses, you will be better equipped to roll with life's surprises. Car break down? No problem. Unexpected vet bill? You've got this. Very little will be able to rock you to your core.

Step 4—Refinance all other debt (student loans, mortgage, car) to a lower rate and shorter term. For student loans, mortgages, and car loans, shop around to pay the lowest rate for the shortest term. It's always a win if you can pay off debt in seven years instead of ten years with just a small increase in your monthly payment.

Step 5—Invest for the long term. Up to this point, you've changed your diet, lost some weight, and improved your range of motion. Now, it's time to test your physical and mental limits. It's time for a marathon.

The financial equivalent to running a marathon is investing for the long run. We introduced this in Step 1 as it relates to your 401(k) and company match, but now it's time to contribute more than your company match.

If your company doesn't offer a 401(k), open an Individual Retirement Account (IRA). You can contribute up to $6,000 in 2019. Like your 401(k), an IRA is a tax-free retirement fund. You can open an IRA at any online brokerage firm.

After retirement accounts are funded, you can now open a regular brokerage account and invest the money you've saved from giving yourself a raise!

Step 6—Saving for short-term and intermediate-term goals. Short-term and intermediate-term goals include things like vacations, events, experiences, and down payments. When you get to this point, you should have many of the basics covered, and you can have some fun!

PUTTING IT ALL TOGETHER

Think of these steps as part of your wealth-building machine. The machine is always running, and you need to make sure the parts are moving in sync. Aggressively paying down student loans, but racking up credit card debt? Something's wrong. You need to take care of the credit card debt first. Going on amazing vacations but have no savings? One unexpected disruption will hurt you financially. Have a brokerage account, but don't participate in your company's 401(k) plan? You're missing out on free money. Most people will never know if you're financially fit, and that's okay because one very important person will know. The person that's impossible to fool—you.

Conclusion

Ding, dong! Knock, knock, knock.

I open the door. A bag of Chinese food is waiting for us on the other side.

"Thank you!" I say, and I walk toward the kitchen. And now, that dreaded feeling. I thought I was able to bury it when placing the order, and I was convinced that it would lie dormant for the night, but it's here, and it wants its presence to be known.

"Oh, hello, shame! Haven't seen you in a while! Welcome to our home this evening."

This happened last weekend. Yes, we broke a money (and health) rule. Unhealthy food ordered from a restaurant that's within a five-minute walk from our apartment. Delivery fee and tip paid for no good reason. All for unhealthy and overpriced food that provides minimal value. So, why did we do it? Why did we violate the principles highlighted in this book? Because we're f*!&ing humans! This is what we do.

But here's the thing—a few years ago, this was a nightly event. Another unintentional food choice. Allowing ourselves to feed into the excuse that we don't have time to shop and cook. It was more than just food. It was clothes, cars, jewelry—you name it.

This is no longer who we are. We made a choice to bring awareness to our consumption, to take accountability for what we want, and to take deliberate action toward defining and achieving our goals. We did the deep work, and now one unintentional decision is just that. One mistake. A minor transgression. It doesn't define us. And we can leave it where it is and move on. All because we made a choice to take control and drive our relationship with money, instead of allowing money to drive us.

So far, our wealth-building journey has been a lot of fun. We rarely go to expensive restaurants (or eat out at all), new clothes are a rare treat (or born out of necessity), and the random impulse purchases are pretty much nonexistent. But we've traveled the world, increased our spending on wellness experiences, and saved up enough capital to start our own business. All because we brought meaning and intention to the process.

Your wealth-building journey is unlikely to start with an epiphany. The only way you will experience the meaning, purpose, and freedom that comes with financial independence is if you decide that you want it. Wealth is a choice. Are you ready for it? Are you tired of making other people rich? If so, don't wait for inspiration to strike. Instead, take action the moment you finish this book. Pay off $25 of your credit card balance, move $100 to a savings account, build a budget, track last week's expenses, create a savings game, start a side hustle, or schedule an appointment with a wealth coach. Do anything you can do to take the first step right now. Wealth and abundance are waiting for you.

Accountability Exercises (Guides)

FUTURE YOU WEALTH
SAVE, INVEST, AND SPEND WITH INTENTION

What Do You Want?

Your Name:

Date:

WANT #1:

- What needs to happen to satisfy this want?
- Am I fulfilling any parts of this want?
- What is getting in my way (money can be included)?
- Why am I letting it?
- Are the roadblocks insurmountable? If not, how can I navigate around them?
- What will life look like if I do nothing?
- If I work toward this want, how will I feel?

FUTURE YOU WEALTH
SAVE, INVEST, AND SPEND WITH INTENTION

The Detachment Framework

Your Name:

Date:

STEP 1

Write out a description of the main character in a book, TV show, or movie that you most admire.

Next, answer the following questions:

- Who are they (write their bio)?
- What are their strengths?
- What are their weaknesses?
- What makes them special?

- What are their flaws?
- Why do you respect them?
- How do their material things or possessions influence the way you think about them?
- What attracts you to them?
- What are their attachments, and how are they a disservice to the character?

STEP 2

Repeat this same process, but for a character that you most despise. A villain, nemesis, or cheater.

Answer the following questions:

- Who are they (write their bio)?
- What are their strengths?
- What are their weaknesses?
- What are their flaws?
- How do their material things or possessions influence the way you think about them?
- What do you find unattractive about them?
- Next, write down his or her attachments.

STEP 3

Repeat this process for yourself.

- Who are you (write your bio)?
- What are your strengths?
- What are your weaknesses?
- What are your flaws?
- What role do material things play in your life?
- What are your attachments? How are they holding you back?

STEP 4

Repeat this process for the future version of you.

FUTURE YOU WEALTH
SAVE, INVEST, AND SPEND WITH INTENTION

Wealth on Your Terms

Your Name:

Date:

Define your level of wealth for each category below:

- Time:
- Unconditional Love:
- Knowledge:
- Adventure:
- Health:

FUTURE YOU WEALTH
SAVE, INVEST, AND SPEND WITH INTENTION

What Are You Willing to Commit To?

Your Name:

Date:

- What do I want?
- What am I willing to commit to?
- What vulnerabilities am I willing to embrace?
- What is my benchmark for success?
- Why does committing to this want make me proud?

Acknowledgments

I must start by thanking my incredible wife, Lauren. There is no way this book could have been written without you. From late-night edits, to emotional support, to your unconditional love, you were in this every step of the way. I can't wait for our next chapter together.

Thank you to Cali. You have an amazing ability to put everything in perspective. Your positive energy, excitement, and love were needed throughout this journey.

Thank you to my family. Words cannot describe how much I value your support, feedback, encouragement, and, most importantly, your unconditional love.

Thank you to Hal Clifford, Emily Gindlesparger, Nicole Jobe, and Tucker Max for your support, guidance, and honest (and sometimes difficult) feedback. You all made me feel uncomfortable at times, but I am grateful that you were willing to "hurt my feelings" in order to make this book the best it could be.

Thank you to my former self for disarming your ego and committing to change.

About the Author

RYAN STERLING is the founder and head wealth coach at Future You Wealth. He has over fifteen years of experience helping individuals and families achieve their financial goals in addition to teaching financial literacy courses in underserved communities. He has a BA in economics from Carleton College, an MBA with a specialization in investment management from Vanderbilt University, and is a CFA® Charterholder. When not working or writing for the Future You Wealth blog, you can find Ryan running along the Hudson River, playing basketball, or hanging out in lower Manhattan with his amazing wife, Lauren, and their energetic pup, Cali.

Disclaimer

This book is sold with the understanding that the author is not offering individualized advice to any individual's specific circumstances. A professional opinion should be sought if one needs customized advice on any financial planning, investment, legal, or tax matter. While this book references historical returns and hypothetical situations, past results do not guarantee future performance. The data highlighted in this book is used as a guide to highlight some of the book's principles. All views, expressions, and opinions included in this communication are subject to change. This communication is not intended as an offer or solicitation to buy, hold, or sell any financial instrument or investment advisory services. Any information provided has been obtained from sources considered reliable, but we do not guarantee the accuracy, or the completeness of, any description of securities, markets, or developments mentioned. The author disclaims any responsibility for any liability or loss incurred as a consequence of the use and application of any of the contents in this book.

Made in the USA
Monee, IL
28 December 2020

54625667R10128